STAND

Overcoming
a *Lifetime*
of abuse and neglect
with GRACE
and DIGNITY

DEBRA SUE BASS-WILLIAMSON
CO-WRITTEN BY CARON GOODE

SOUPER PUBLISHING
SANDY, UT

Published by:
Souper Publishing
8042 Hunters Meadow Circle
Sandy, UT 84093 USA

978-0-9801234-0-1   0-9801234-0-2

Printed in the United States of America.

Library of Congress Cataloging-in-Publication Data
is available from the publisher.

For My Knight,

Your love has taught me patience, forgiving, understanding and true strength. You have been there every step of the way with open arms. You have loved me unconditionally and held me up when I could not stand on my own. I will be forever at your side.

ACKNOWLEDGEMENTS

Thank you, Mom, your unconditional love and intuitive sight made this possible. I will be forever grateful for your lessons and your faith, for without them I would not be where I am today.

Caron all my heart, without your skill of writing and your advice this would not have been possible. Thank you.

Evan, my buddy, my sister—your friendship has driven me. And yes, I felt like a used car for much too long.

Aunt Betty, thank you for filling in where Mom could not. You are always in my heart.

My children—Shawn, Wendy, Katy and Nancy—your every breath has made my life a continuous miracle.

Gary, my husband, my best friend—thank you for always being there no matter where there happens to be.

Grandma, thank you for your visits from the other side and for your guidance.

Thank you, God! The gifts I have received have made me who I am.

CONTENTS

Dear Children,

I am sorry for:
the horrible fighting you had to endure.
the hurt you saw me inflict upon your father.
the neglect you received.
running away when things got bad.
being mean and unbearable.
not being there when you needed me most.
not making sure you received enough love.

Most of all I am sorry for not taking a stand and loving the person I am. I am telling you this now because I watch you make the same choices that I did.

You can learn from your parents' choices instead of making them your own. You can learn to believe in who you are instead of being afraid of your gifts.

Your childhood was not your fault. You learned what not to be, and now you will show my grandchildren how to love who they are because you can love yourselves. I want my grandchildren to live in homes where they are loved and valued, where they can make happy childhood memories.

For my daughters, I want you to honor your own beauty, to believe in yourself. Each of you is a beautiful woman. I want you to have love and to know with all your heart that you are worthy of this love. Teach your daughters the same.

My son, I want you to recognize your heart's strength. I want you to honor the love you receive by believing in yourself. Be loyal to yourself; to your own self be true. I want you to teach my grandsons this by living it. Most of all I want you to know that I do not regret the choices I made in the circumstances of my life. They were necessary for me to learn, grow and heal. I believe that everything happens for a reason, and that is why I am writing this now.

The future is your choice each day of your life.

INTRODUCTION

$\mathscr{T}$he details of my suicide were planned right down to the final moment. I envisioned it clearly. On the appointed evening, I would drive home from work as usual, pick up speed, aim for the large oak tree that was near the shoulder of the road by my house and crash head on.

Everyone would believe it was an accident. My children would never know that I did it intentionally. I would be free at last. No more would I have to live my life.

That was my glorified version of how to step out of this life; it did not happen.

Instead, I swallowed a bottle of sleeping pills and went to bed one afternoon. I woke up in the emergency room drinking charcoal. My daughter had found me and called her dad to tell him she couldn't wake me up.

After that event, the ultimate shame hovered over me like a swarm of bees. The constant buzzing relentlessly reminded me of what I had just done to my children.

Two days after I got home from the hospital I called a friend who recommended a self-help program. Two weeks later, I was on my way to Boise, Idaho for what turned out to be a life-saving event. From that point forward, I began to live my life. Do you ever wonder *how* you got to where you are in life? And then wondered *why* you made the choices you did? I've asked myself these questions most of my adult life. I finally figured it out for myself, and my story has a happy ending.

My story includes three generations of abominable abuse of the darkest variety: sexual, emotional, and mental. My story sheds light on the shadow side of the adult human that uses children to relieve his sexual appetites and need for power and domination over the innocent and helpless. But my story ends in triumph instead of despair.

Being raped and sexually abused as a child imprisoned me in a lifetime of emotional and mental anguish. Not only did I survive and heal those emotional and spiritual wounds, I found great happiness. I want to share the how and why with you.

We all have a story to tell and I am hoping mine will make a difference to someone out there. It is my hope that you won't feel alone or think of yourself as another tragic statistic that dreams of leaving by the back door of suicide as I once did.

Yes, I wrote this story to give you hope because it is an inspirational and triumphant coming-of-age memoir. I also wrote it for my children, that they might recognize the miracles that have been bestowed upon us and stop this sickening cycle of abuse.

1

STOLEN INNOCENCE
1965

Courage takes many forms. There is physical courage, there is moral courage. Then there is still a higher courage—the courage to brave pain, to live with it, to never let others know of it, and to still find joy in life; to wake up in the morning with an enthusiasm for the day ahead.
—Howard Cosell

*M*y sister, my cousin and I spent a hot summer day in the pool and were spending the night at our Uncle Sam's house. It was supposed to be another carefree day spent with family, celebrating the summer vacation. Instead, it was the day that my life started sliding down a steep and treacherous hill. That night, my twenty-two year old uncle walked into our room and told me that I was noisy and had to sleep in his room with him.

Immediately, I got a sick feeling in my stomach, but at nine years old, I didn't know what it was, just that something was very wrong. With the innocence of a child who had been taught to obey my elders, I walked into his darkened bedroom and climbed into his bed. The sheets smelled like alcohol and I was very afraid.

When he crawled in to bed next to me, I could feel his hairy leg on my skin. He was naked. I had never been next to anybody with hairy legs and I grew more confused and terrified.

I tried to shrink inside myself. I tried to hide. My body became stiff and my hands were drenched in sweat. Tears threatened to fall, but I tried to hold them back.

Sam put his hand on my stomach and shook me.

"Debbie, are you awake?"

I pretended not to hear him and acted like I was sleeping. When I felt him slide my pajama bottoms off my body, I was frozen with fear and kept quiet because I didn't know what to do.

I tried to roll over to get away from him, like I was tossing in my sleep, but he pulled me back over to him. He took off my underwear and I almost threw up.

I fought back the lump in my throat, knowing that I was going to throw up or cry or scream. His hands were all over me, pushing my legs apart. He grabbed my hand and put it on his penis.

What the heck is that?

I knew he was a boy, and that his body was different from mine, but that was the extent of my knowledge as a frightened nine-year-old girl. I didn't know what I was feeling and I was terrified of him, of it, and of the whole situation.

He just kept touching me. He was rubbing me between my legs and I didn't like it. He whispered words I didn't understand. He rolled on top of me.

He was crushing me. I couldn't breathe.

"Debbie, are you awake? Debbie?"

I kept my eyes closed tight and didn't say a word. He penetrated me, and I could feel the pain—a burst of intense heat. He was ripping my guts open. I was blacking out. It hurt so badly and I didn't want to be in my own body. He penetrated me.

He did.

I remember trying to breathe and telling myself that Sam couldn't hurt me. I remember thinking that he'd go away. I started praying quietly as the tears silently started to fall.

I couldn't move. I couldn't scream because I was too scared. I couldn't open my eyes, I couldn't breathe. There's nothing to scream. More tears were coming out, and I couldn't fight them back anymore. I was scared that if he knew I was awake I was going be in trouble, but the tears just kept coming.

I don't remember what happened next. It hurt so bad that I still can't remember. I may have blacked out because I remember thinking that my legs weren't attached to my body anymore. They felt like they were gone. I could feel the pain, but it was as though they weren't there anymore.

It felt awful. It felt wrong. It felt sickening. He moved away and wasn't on me anymore. He was lying beside me with his hand on my stomach, but I still couldn't move.

"Debbie, are you awake?"

I never answered him and I never opened my eyes. I just laid there pretending to sleep, all the long night, quietly frozen in fear until I could see the light come through the curtains.

Debbie

When I got up in the morning my knees wobbled and there was blood dripping down my legs. It felt like I had peed my pants, but not.

Sam was still sleeping as I snuck quietly out of his room and made my way to the bathroom as fast as I could. I found a washrag to clean myself and get dressed. To this day, I don't remember ever being so scared. I didn't want to tell anybody. I didn't know what to do, but I wanted to hide from the world and be alone.

When I walked outside, everybody was out by the pool.

My uncle yelled at me, "Get your swimming suit on. Everybody's swimming."

"I don't want to."

But because of the way he looked at me, and the authoritarian tone of his voice, I went and put on my swimsuit. I didn't wash myself any more because I felt like my body was on fire with pain.

It actually felt good to get in the pool and stop the burning. It hurt to walk. I couldn't take big steps. I couldn't play.

All I knew was that Sam had done something to me and I was afraid I was going to die. I stayed in the water for a long time. The longer I stayed in the pool, the better it felt. My uncle swam over to me later and cornered me in the deep end.

"I need to talk to you."

I felt sick to my stomach and I thought I was going to vomit. I wanted to scream and cry. I didn't want my sister to leave me alone with him.

He pushed me under the water and held me under. I gasped for air, clawing at his hand that held me down. When he finally let me up, he said, "You have to promise me you won't tell anybody what happened."

"What are you talking about? I don't know what you're talking about. I don't know what you mean. You mean trying to drown me?"

"No, you know what I mean." He pushed me back under the water.

I did know what he meant the first time. Did he know I was awake and faking sleep? After the fourth time, gasping for breath and shaking with fear, I promised him I would never tell.

Sam told my sister and cousin to go inside and eat lunch. He told them we were talking because I'd gotten in trouble and needed to be disciplined. They left me in that pool with him. I was so afraid of him, I hated him and was incapable of understanding what had happened. Sam was my favorite uncle; I couldn't believe he had done that to me.

I blamed myself for what had happened. I truly believed that I had done something bad and the assault was my fault. I was consumed by guilt and thought that I was some kind of a horrible child. Was I too loud? Was I too noisy? Why had he chosen to hurt me? Was I bad?

My uncle told me not to say anything to anyone. He promised

that if I were quiet from then on, it wouldn't ever happen again. I never said a word.

When I finally got home, I went to my room and stayed there alone. I didn't talk to my family. I didn't play with my cousin or my sister. I hid under my bed and tried to be really quiet. I believed that if I were really quiet, I wouldn't get in trouble. The shame of what had happened consumed me, but even though I wanted to tell on him, I was too afraid.

My mom came in to find me just as it was starting to get dark outside.

"You have to go stay at your uncle's again." I started to cry, but I couldn't tell her why. .

I desperately wanted to stay home that night but with so many relatives in town, Sam told my mom we could stay with him for another night rather than in our overcrowded house.

Still, I hid under that bed hoping I wouldn't have to go.

"Come out from underneath that bed, Debbie. You guys are leaving."

I still couldn't speak up. I couldn't come out from under the bed. . I was afraid that if I said something I'd get in trouble. As my mom pulled me out from under the bed by my leg, I hung onto the bedpost, afraid to let go and go back.

"If you don't get your butt out in that car, I'm gonna beat your ass."

My nine-year-old self just kept telling me:

You'll be all right. Just be real quiet and don't say a word all night long and you won't get in trouble. He won't make me sleep in his room again.

When my sister, cousin and I arrived in front of our uncle's door, I bit my lip, trying to hold back my vomit. But I couldn't hold back. The tears and the vomit came as I ran to the bathroom to be sick. I couldn't quit throwing up.

My uncle beat on the door and yelled "You need to knock it off or I'm gonna call your mom."

When I came out of the bathroom, Sam took me to his room and that was it. There was no pretending to be asleep this time. I didn't cry or say anything. I kept silent while he hurt me repeatedly. It was the same pain, only longer. I didn't think he'd ever get off me. I remember just trying to get a breath during what seemed like an eternity of being crushed. I blanked in and out, seemingly not sleeping all night.

The next morning, I got out of bed quietly and wiped off my legs the way I did the morning before. I thought I was going to bleed to death. This was the second morning that I had locked myself in the bathroom to wipe the blood away from my legs. I'd never seen myself bleed before, and I was scared that I was dying.

I was very careful to rinse the washrag out so my sister wouldn't go in and brush her teeth and see it. She was younger than I, and the thought of her enduring my uncle's abuse made me more angry than afraid. Thinking of my younger sister, I marched into the kitchen and told my uncle, "If you ever touch my sister, I'll tell on you." I don't know where that came from.

"Okay. We're going to go swim."

"I'm not going to swim." I had found my voice.

I sat in a chair in the corner and watched everyone else swim. My uncle never touched me again. And, I never uttered a word about what had happened for the next six years.

2

THE LEGACY OF GENERATIONS
1900-1948

"Evil (ignorance) is like a shadow—it has no real substance of its own, it is simply a lack of light. You cannot cause a shadow to disappear by trying to fight it, stamp on it, by railing against it, or any other form of emotional or physical resistance. In order to cause a shadow to disappear, you must shine light on it."—Shakti Gawain

My Grandma Bessie grew up in Vernal, Utah. In fact, her mother was one of the Utah pioneers who traveled here for a new beginning. It's funny how the world plays tricks on us. As a child of the early 1900s, Grandma was raised to be obedient and to always know her place. Her father raised her with a strong hand and a lot of humility.

As a child, Bessie worked from sun up to sun down on the family's farm. She taught herself to read and write in her spare time, which often was in the middle of the night, as they were not allowed to go to school. When Bessie was fifteen years old, her father arranged a marriage between her and a local boy named Clarence. Although it was an arranged marriage, Bessie fell in love with Clarence and he with her. They moved from Vernal, Utah to Park City where Clarence had a job in the mines and Bessie worked as a hair-

Bessie Alice Glen

dresser in a local hotel beauty salon. They soon started a family and their firstborn were twin girls. They then had a boy a few years later. Bessie worked as hard at being a good mother and wife as she did at her part time job as a hairdresser. When her youngest child was three, Clarence was in a mining accident and died.

Although her father had picked her husband, Bessie loved Clarence very much. They had a good life together. Clarence respected and loved Bessie. He encouraged her to work at a local beauty salon until she had enough experience to open her own shop. He promised her he would help build her a shop in front of their home in the front porch sunroom. Bessie was devastated when he was killed. Her heart was broken, but she was a strong woman and had three small children to take care of. She remained focused on her dreams, confident that Clarence would watch over her.

Bessie tried to work more hours and provide for her children, but in time she was forced to move back home with her parents, who helped her with her small children while she worked and continued

Bessie and Clarence

her schooling. Bessie finished beauty school and finally realized her dream of operating her own shop from her small home where she could work and be a mom. She had found peace with Clarence's death and was living life on her own terms.

Bessie believed in being honest and kind to everyone. She treated everyone in town with respect—even the prostitutes who would come to her shop. She built a business and worked hard to provide for her children, while being kind and generous to those she crossed paths with.

Bessie had been a widow for nine years when she met George at a dance over the holidays. He was very charming and lavished her with attention before finally proposing marriage. Eleven months after their first date, with George promising to take care of Bessie and her children, they married.

Shortly after George and Bessie married, they started a family together. They had six children together and, along with the three Grandma Bessie had with Clarence, they had nine kids to support. My mom was the youngest of the nine. Grandma Bessie was thirty-seven when my mother was born and George was forty-eight.

In the beginning of the new marriage, George was very good to Bessie. They worked together to raise their children and build a new life together. After a couple of years, however, George started to change. It started with him telling Grandma how stupid and incapable she was and it only got worse. George had very strict religious beliefs and those beliefs, combined with his emerging alcohol abuse, caused her life to quickly spiral out of Bessie's control.

George Goodrich

Bessie worked long hours to avoid George whenever possible. He raped her when he felt the need and told her she was evil for enticing him. He would then punish her by reading for hours on end from the Bible and making her repeat what he had read. Bessie was afraid to leave him because George told her he would kill her.

She went to her parents for help, but they told her as a God-fearing Christian woman, it was her responsibility to obey her husband and she was never to come to them with such ridiculous complaints and accusations. Her father warned her that if she did, she would never be welcome in their home again, that no daughter of his would ever make up such lies.

Bessie did as her father ordered, and the circle of abuse continued. George's abuse of his children started the minute they were born. He would preach from the Bible for five hours every Sunday night at the dinner table and tell his family that God had seen the evil in each of them and that they would all burn in hell. George belittled his children, beat them and, as they grew older, sexually abused them. Lois

George and Lois

was special. She was her daddy's princess. She had to try even harder to do *exactly* what God and Daddy wanted . . .

Thirteen-year-old Betty walks home on the quiet street in Maeser, Utah, towing her younger six-year-old sister Lois. Lois was a beautiful child with thick brunette hair and rosy cheeks, but she never felt beautiful next to her popular, blonde-haired lovely sister. Any neighbor would notice that they walk with their heads down and they don't smile or gab much.

The girls were in a funk because they weren't looking forward to entering the empty house into which they'd recently moved. Their mom was at work and their dad, George, could be anywhere. They were hopeful that he was not at home, but instead was hanging out with his cronies in town. They had learned early on to purposefully avoid the ranting man who was their father by fate's design.

They made their way through the gate of the white picket fence, up the narrow cement walk to their front door. They entered the 150 square-foot living room, and put their schoolwork on a small phone table behind the door so their mother could review it later.

"Lois, why don't you go see if you can find a snack in the kitchen? I'm going to rest a while."

Betty hated the new house, the new school, her loneliness, her mother working a beautician's hours to support nine children, her lunatic father, teasing brothers and the rest of the "stuff" that went on in the house that no one talked about. In her private quiet bedroom, she slipped between cool sheets. She shared the bedroom and its bunk beds with Lois, although Betty thought of the room as hers. Helplessness and tears washed over her as she thought about little Lois. *It wasn't her fault; her mother wouldn't listen to her; what could she do?*

Betty hid her face under a pillow and tried to sleep through her tears, as she did most days. *Maybe she'd feed Lois dinner later, if she could find anything to feed her.*

Lois got her pink diary and went into the kitchen. Pausing for a moment, she considered a snack but realized that there would be nothing to eat today as there wasn't anything yesterday. Her gaze wandered to her hiding spot behind the small, white, square coal-burning stove. The stove sat catty corner to the wall, providing a

Hopscotch Valley...

IN LOVE

By Lois Marie Goodrich

I am in love;
I'm sure of it
And if I were a queen,
I'd marry now
Because I know
A brave and fine marine.

I'd go with him
Across the sea
To work for Uncle Sam,
And soon my friends
Would know for sure
How much in love I am.

—*Jingle by Anna Johnson.*

Lois Marie is the daughter of
Mr. and Mrs. Geo. R. Goodrich

Lois Marie

cozy space for Lois and her small stool. She read, wrote, thought and hid from her family in the cubbyhole. The natural light from the window above allowed reading after school; the slots in the coal-burning stove shed enough reading light into the evening hours. She's safe here, she thinks. Lois crawled into her slot between the small kitchen sink and stove. Leaning against the corner where the two walls met, she sat on her stool and opened her diary. Here she could talk to the pages awaiting her heart's words.

> *Dear Diary,*
> *I'm hungry and Betty is asleep. I hope Daddy never comes home.*
> *He'll do that awful stuff to me, and it hurts. I'm going to sleep here*

now. Ohh, I'm so hungry, when I grow up I will live in a big beautiful house with tons of food. It will be so fun. And it will always be warm, not dark and cold like here.

Neither Betty nor Lois noticed that evening had come. Mom hadn't come home yet, but their dad did.

In fact, George staggered into their living room and flopped in his favorite chair. "Helloooooo!" He thinks he is shouting to his family, but his voice is barely a whisper, so disparate is his hearing in his drunken state.

Lois

"Where's my little dooooolll?"

Because nobody was around, Daddy went to the kitchen, looking for Lois. He knew where she was, but he called for her anyway, giving her a chance to obey him and get his approval. "Lois, come to Daddy."

Lois' daddy knew that she would eventually come out. She was his little girl and deep down, she craved his approval. He'd told her that God wanted her to do special things with Daddy and that if she didn't, God wouldn't love her anymore.

But still, Lois remained quiet.

"Lois, come to Daddy."

"Now, Lois." The tenor of his voice deepened, finally moving Lois into action.

She crept quietly from her hiding space, leaving her diary there because she knew she'd eventually be back—hiding again.

"Hi, Daddy," she murmured, with her head down. He smiled

14

sweetly at her and stroked her hair like she was his favorite dog. "How's Daddy's beautiful little girl?" he slurs. "Come with Daddy."

George took her by the hand and into the warmth of the darkened master bedroom. Odors of sex and sweat hung on the drapes and messy sheets. Lois' frightened legs refuse to take another step and her Daddy lifted her up and laid her gently on the bed

"Daddy's sweet girl. Daddy's baby girl is so beautiful. Yes, she is." he cooed. George fluffed her pillow and tucked the covers around her. Next, he undressed himself and climbed into bed beside his baby girl. His index finger stroked her cheeks and wiped away the tear rolling down her cheek. Two of his fingers twirled the bits of her hair resting on the pillow. Such games were Daddy's foreplay.

Lois can't remember the first time Daddy took her into that bedroom. She's not sure how old she was when it started. She never spoke of that first time with Daddy—ever.

She stiffened her body in anticipation of her daddy's next move. She closed her eyes and shrunk within herself. It was time to go away and talk to the angels because what Daddy did to her hurt so badly. George absently hummed a melody while playing with his baby—his youngest daughter. He stroked her chest and rubbed her tummy, slowly moving downward in the familiar path of her body. His two fingers spread her thin legs apart.

Daddy lost any sense of time or any familiarity with the pretty plaything which he continued petting. His flaccid penis would harden and the sexual rush would consume him. He would enter the child, barely penetrating, yet pushing again and again until he was satisfied. *Such a sweet baby, little Lois. Daddy's girl.*

Lois would smile at her angels, as she always seemed to do when she was with them. She started playing with them when she was just four and she loved to visit their fairyland full of colorful flower arrays, pastoral fields and light that glimmered everywhere. Her

angels played with her and helped her understand that life would be better when she grew up. Actually, Lois knew the angels were always with her because she felt their loving warmth and listened to their wise encouragement.

When Lois would return to her body after visiting the angels, she would turn away from Daddy and silently weep into her pillow. The lower half of her slender body burned so badly; she was paralyzed. She would lie still, praying to her angels to lift her up again into the space of painlessness.

When she would awake to the reality of her life, she would sneak out of her snoring Daddy's bed and make her way to her cubbyhole, grabbing a quilt from the bed first.

Dear Diary,
I hate Daddy. I wish he were dead. I wish I could be with angels all the time. Where's Mommy?

The truth was, Mommy never came to check on Lois. No one did. After she snuck out of Daddy's bed, Lois would snuggle in her quilt in her special place and fall asleep to the warmth of the coal stove. The next morning, when she would awake to hear Betty and her brothers getting ready for school, she would run to the bathroom to clean her self up. After dressing and grabbing some soda crackers from the kitchen cupboard, she would run out the door in time to walk to school with Betty and her brothers.

After a night with Daddy, when Lois would enter her classroom, her teacher always greeted her warmly, attempting to brush the unkempt hair from her face.

"And how is Lois this morning?"

"Okay," replied Lois, staring at her shoes.

"Lois, are you all right? Did you get some sleep last night?"

"Yes."

The teacher would kneel down in front of Lois and cup her chin, gently lifting her face to see her eyes. "Lois, I am your friend. If you need help, you can tell me. Is there anything wrong at home?"

"No."

"All right, then. Let's have a good day today, shall we?"

"Hmmm . . . " Lois would hum as she slipped away to her desk and chair. As much as she was afraid of her dad, Lois loved him. She was his princess. If she told anyone, it would take away the special relationship she had with him. So she said nothing at all.

Lois was closest in age to her brothers, Merl, who was three and half years older, and Marv, who was five years older. The three shared normal growing up discoveries and curiosities like playing "doctor" or "mom and dad." Other shared moments included taking the cow out to the pasture, spending hot summer afternoons in the cooler tree house where Marv and his sister shared lunches of sandwiches, fresh tomatoes, or canned fruit.

Her older brother, Phil, was not her friend. Like his father before him, the abuse cycle continued as he molested Lois as well.

Phil was seventeen years old, ten years older than Lois. He molested her every day in the shed out back of the house. Phil offered Lois dimes, nickels, and quarters to practice oral sex on her. Lois liked the money because she could buy treats that she would not have otherwise. This was the only time she felt warmth or closeness from any older sibling, and she could visit her angels at the same time. Lois thought it was love—her daddy taught her that.

Only years later did Lois understand Phil didn't love her; rather, he coerced her into this sick intimate relationship. She cried with relief when she finally understood that she was not a prostitute, and the relationship was not her fault in those tender years of ages six through nine.

3

CHAOS BEGETS CHAOS
1948–1953

"A life lived in chaos is an impossibility . . . "—Madeleine L'Engle

L ois matured and continued to endure abuse at the hand of her father and older brother, Phil. In addition to her angels, Lois also coped with the pain by escaping into the world of books. Reading became her free ticket to exotic lands and provided a glimpse into the lives of other characters. And because of her continuing love of the written word, her diary became her best friend.

Dear Diary,
My eighth birthday is over. I read a book about another girl who is like me. Her parents were divorcing. I cried all night because I felt her pain. Her family was torn apart by the choices they had to make.

"Lois Marie, get your nose out of that damn book and put on your glasses."

Lois' mother spat out remarks like this throughout the day when she was home, interrupting Lois' concentration. Too many late nights of reading behind the coal stove caused her eyestrain. She soon required reading glasses, which she regularly forgot to wear. Her mother would hound her to remember. During her mother's yelling bouts, Lois often longed to be neither seen nor heard. Her greatest joy would be to shrink inside herself, disappear into her book and try to be invisible from her mother.

When Lois was eight years old, she moved into a two-bedroom apartment in Vernal with her mom and dad. The apartment was on the second floor in the commercial area of town, above a doctor's office and a saloon, not a place where a woman would go. The saloon had a large parlor with a linoleum floor, several chairs and a straight stiff couch. There were several parlors off of the main room, and

Lois

four more bedrooms, which older men rented occasionally. Lois' mom handled the rentals in exchange for rent.

Lois' sisters Eunice and Eulla were married and starting their families about the time Lois was born. Lois' interests were better aligned with her nieces and nephews. She often played with them when she was young and she babysat for them when she was older.

Lois' brother Dee had moved out long before Lois was born, to enter the service. When he returned, he married and started his family. When the family moved into the apartment, twins Larry and Phil also left home–to join the service. Merl was put into foster care because of the trouble he was getting into, and Marv was living with a family and working for the husband, but ended up going to the State Reform School for cashing forged checks.

Betty returned that summer from visiting family in New York City, and started working as a waitress at the bus depot diner. She became engaged to her high school sweetheart, and eventually married. Lois would sometimes sneak into her sister's closet to try on the beautiful clothes Betty had bought in New York City. She loved the beadwork, embroidery, and brightly colored fabrics of the tailored fashions.

When she was nine years old, Lois bounced around, living with different relatives while her mother sorted out her relationship with Lois' father. George moved out of the smaller apartment early on. Then her father committed the most heinous crime against Lois Marie.

One day Lois was walking home from school and she ran into her father in downtown Vernal. He demanded that she go with him to the parlor where he was a regular visitor. He took her into a small room in the back where there were four men. George told her to do as she was told and he would be back for her.

Three of the men, Lois' father's friends, raped her repeatedly. Her father came to fetch her several hours later, but he made her walk home by herself from there.

The immediate pain of this sexual torture was unbearable. The long-term damage would haunt Lois for the rest of her life. In addition to the emotional turmoil of being prostituted by her father, Lois' reproductive system was permanently damaged as well. At age twenty-nine, she had cervical cancer; during her childbearing years, she suffered four miscarriages; she almost bled to death delivering her third child; and she had to have a hysterectomy at age forty.

Dear Diary,
I feel wise at age ten. Mom said that she was leaving Dad. They are getting a divorce. I am glad. I just want to be with Mom. Dad told me that I would have to talk to the judge for him. Mom accused him of trying to kill her with a butcher knife from the kitchen. I believe Mom. Whenever I see Dad on the street, I avoid him. I'm afraid of him. I am glad Mother is divorcing him. When I grow up and have a family they will be happy and nice to each other. We will play games and hang around on the lawn together.

Lois never did have to testify at her parents' divorce trial. She was relieved when they finally divorced because she felt that her mother and father were each pulling on her, tearing her apart emotionally.

STAND

The next move of this much smaller family, just Mom and Lois, was to Ogden, to live with her mom's brother, Earl and his wife, Lori.

Dear Diary,
I'm awestruck by Uncle Earl. He has a wild sense of humor. I think I'm jealous of the whole family because I fantasize that Uncle Earl is my dad all the time. Uncle Earl laughs a lot, and Aunt Lori seems more serious. She is always proper and polite, but distant emotionally. Uncle Earl is everything my dad wasn't. He works, provides a good living for his family, teases, laughs, loves people and shows it. I just know that someday I will wake up and they will tell me that Uncle Earl is my real father. When I grow up I will marry a man just like him. More tomorrow.

Lois' father brought child neglect charges against her mother while they were still living with Uncle Earl and Aunt Lori. Lois and her parents met in the judge's chambers, and the judge asked Lois point blank if she wanted to live with her father.

"No" was her only reply because she knew she would run away if her father gained custody.

Dear Diary,
I know Mom and Dad are divorced, but it seems to me that they never got divorced at all. They just changed their living arrangements.

While Lois stayed at Uncle Earl's house, her mom had a brief foray of living with Jim Campbell for a few months. When Jim became physically violent with Lois' mom, she told him to leave, and that was the end of their relationship. While Lois was happy and secure in Uncle Earl's home, her mom was still confused and

22

fighting with Lois' father. When the time came to move out of Uncle Earl's home, Lois was heartbroken. She knew living with her mom was never going to work. She knew she would end up in foster care.

Dear Diary,
Seeing a real father like Uncle Earl makes me wonder why Dad is such a child. Mom said once that he was sick. I'm more like his parent and I know how to control him.

Back with her Mom in the ensuing months, Lois was on her own as a typical latchkey kid who ran the streets and became street-savvy quickly. However she did not fully understand the results of many of her choices. High school boys dragging Washington Boulevard often picked up Lois and her girlfriends and went to the Canyons to drink and party all night. Dangerous older men also prowled Washington Boulevard looking for vulnerable prey in the form of young women like Lois.

Dear Diary,
Last night I was walking home from the bowling alley, around 1:00 AM. Some guy in a trench coat started following me. Boy was I scared! I started running and he chased me all the way to our apartment on 26th. Thank God it is a basement apartment. I leapt into the stairwell and barely got the door opened and inside when he hit the door. No one was home, and I cowered by the door all night long. If we had a phone, I would've called the police.

During the summer of 1949, Lois attended a church camp for girls who were old enough to go into Mutual, which is an organization for young girls in the Church of the Latter Day Saints. The girls rode into the High Uintah Mountains in the back of open trucks with wooden side panels. Lois thrived in the mountain air for a short time. However, when she developed laryngitis by day three of the weeklong camping trip, her summer of sleeping in tents, swimming and hiking came to an abrupt end. Lois' only salvation from the boredom and pain after having a tonsillectomy was Mickey's comforting cuddle and the glorious time to read. While her mom wasn't home in the daytime because of work, she was home most evenings. Tired, as always, from working long hours, Lois' mom was very short tempered and too often let Lois come and go as she pleased. Lois was in trouble at school and with the local shop owners. Without any supervision, she hardly ever made it all day at school and had been caught shoplifting on more than one occasion. She knew she was on borrowed time and eventually someone would force her mom into doing something with her.

Dear Diary,
It's all ending, so it doesn't matter anyway. Mom is putting me back in foster care.

Finally, after years of moving back and forth with her Mom and in and out of foster homes, the judge made Lois a "permanent ward of the state" and placed her in permanent foster care. From that point on, Lois never lived with her mother again. Shortly after Lois returned to foster care, her mom married Raymond Ballard and moved to California. Lois couldn't stand him, nor could Betty. He had "come on" to Betty, who was pregnant with her first child. Lois was thirteen years old when her mother brought Raymond with her to visit Lois in a foster home and explain that she was getting married again and moving to California. Then she said goodbye.

Lois's memory was fuzzy on the details of how many foster homes she passed through. Now and then, she would return to live with relatives, usually Betty and her husband, Jay. Jay came from a more stable family background than did Betty and he had a good job as a typesetter for the Tribune newspaper in the afternoon and evenings.

Dear Diary,
I think I've lost count of the foster homes I've been in. Here on the east side of Salt Lake, these people mostly seem like rich snobs who think they are being so wonderful to throw-away kids like me. This home has so much beautiful furniture, lots of food, with plenty of clothes hanging in big closets. These people go to movies and take vacations. I never had such things. I'm in shock. I'm shy. I don't know how to be comfortable here.

Betty and Lois

Betty and Jay, who were only eighteen and nineteen years old, became foster parents for their siblings when Lois was eleven and Merl was sixteen. Betty and Jay also had Dennis, who was two, and were expecting Darrel next. Sometimes, Jay relaxed by drinking. To add to the messy mixture, Dad would "drop by" to visit Betty and Lois, talking for hours about their Mom and the family problems. This arrangement didn't last. Betty couldn't control Lois, who kept getting in trouble. Dealing with her was causing problems in Jay and Betty's marriage. The decision was made to call the social worker. Merl had already left Betty's home and was on his own. Lois was on her way to another foster home.

Dear Diary,
After the Social Worker left the first time, this foster mom said to me, "Don't get any idea about my son." Right! This homely acne-scarred kid was not my dreamboat, but I've become pretty good friends with him and his sister. That's it for now.

When life got too terribly crazy, Lois would read any book she could find on foreign cultures and travel from the school library. After school, Lois would go to the city library. She loved her only escape. She couldn't wait to get a new book, to read a new story and pretend she was the person in the story.

Lois could never have been able to get lost in romance novels. They bored her and were too predictable. Her taste for exotic adventures stretched her imagination around world history and travel. She absolutely loved politics.

She read about the wars, especially about World War II and the Nazis. Adolph Hitler fascinated Lois, although she was afraid of his evil. Perhaps he reminded her of George?

At another foster home, Lois was allowed to go to her mom's family gathering for their annual July reunion and picnic in one of the beautiful canyons around Ogden. Lois left the grassy flats to hike up a mountain trail when her older brother Phil grabbed her from behind in surprise. He turned her around and positioned her in his arms like a lover. Suddenly, his wife walked into the scene and he abruptly let Lois go. She was relieved, unsure at age twelve how to handle this situation.

But when Phil and his wife moved on, tears came into her eyes, slowly spilling over. Lois didn't like the sexual abuse, but she thought she loved her big brother in the romantic sense. She was a confused and lonely young woman who would soon come to understand her sexual responsiveness and her family's dysfunctions.

Once again Lois moved into a new foster home, but this one was good. Aunt Rose and Uncle Chris were very kind to Lois and welcomed her into their home with open arms. She loved them and in time was like a daughter to them. Chris and Rose Bristol had two boys: Ray, a year older than Lois, and Jimmy, two years older than Lois. Lois was the only girl they had ever had living in their home and the boys grew very fond of her. They looked out for her in school and introduced her to all of their friends. They were big brothers to her and liked it. This was the first family that loved her unconditionally and she loved them. Glen lived next door to them, along with his mother, stepfather and his brothers on the family farm. Glen was Chris and Rose's nephew. The boys were always over to Glen's place hanging out and soon, so was Lois. She would follow Glen

Lois

around after school helping him with his chores when he would let her, and watching him work the fields. Lois liked Glen–he was nice to her and he was very attractive. They spent their evenings together on the porch drinking lemonade and talking about the future and where they wanted to be. As time went by they grew very fond of one another and spent all of their free time together.

Dear Diary,

I think my Social Worker wants to get me out of the city to keep me from running away from foster homes. Probably smart. Rose and Chris Bristol accepted me without looking down their noses at me like all the others. Sure, Rose wants help around the house, but they make me feel as if I'm really part of the family. Aunt Rose even hoped I would end up marrying Jimmy, but he's like a brother to me, not a boyfriend. But there is a physical attraction between Glen and me.

4

GRABBING FOR HAPPINESS
1953–1966

May you live all the days of your life.—Jonathan Swift

*G*len and Lois took their marriage vows on October 10, 1953 at the home of Glen's brother, Rex. Lois, four months shy of sixteen years, asked her father to sign the permission papers. Glen was eighteen and admitted he felt pushed into the marriage by his stepfather and his mother and perhaps also by Lois. However, he'll be the first to admit that over time he learned to love Lois dearly.

Lois' driving desire for marriage was to have her own home and family, and not to be "fostered" any more. In her innocent heart, combined with her street-savvy attitudes, Lois engaged Glen in a romantic and sexually active relationship that would keep him interested. Then she thought she might be pregnant.

Dear Diary,

We are living with Glen's Mom, in the basement of her home in Bluffdale. What a joy! There are 2 1/2 bedrooms for Glen and I, his Mom, and three brothers. We share a bedroom with Boyd and Kent, who is a year older than me. Meantime, I am pregnant now, again, after that first miscarriage back in January of '53. I wonder what those twins would have been?

Glen's new stepfather, Alma, finally managed to get Glen hired at Kennecott Copper. Glen worked long hours on the graveyard shift, which was hard for Lois, but this allowed them to get out on their own. Glen and Lois moved out of his mom's home late in 1954. Their second floor apartment on West Temple and 9th seemed like a large place, even though it was just two small rooms and a kitchen. In the meantime, Glen bought and paid off a 1948 Desoto, later trading up to a fast, snazzy, two-door 1950 red Ford.

Glen and Lois felt like they were doing all right even though they were too innocent to realize many of the building's occupants were prostitutes. Three "older" women and their several children lived across the hall from them; they often passed each other on the one-person narrow staircase that led to both apartments. This wasn't easy for Lois, now eight months pregnant with their first child. Although it wasn't the home they had always dreamed of, it was theirs and they were happy.

Dear Diary,

It's been a while, hasn't it? I am so glad to be home from the hospital, but I miss baby Dell so much. He can't come home yet. Dell was born a "blue baby" because of the incompatibility factor of my RH- blood and Glen's RH+ blood. Right after Dell's birth, Dr. Johnson and a pediatric specialist who flew in wanted me to sign papers so they could do a blood exchange on him. They moved me out of the delivery room and whisked Dell off to the nursery. I didn't get to hold him or see him at all. I cried and cried and didn't get to see my baby until he was two days old. I was scared, wondered if he was dead, worried and wanted to call Glen who was out working. No one told me how the transfusion went. When I finally saw Dr. Johnson, he took immediate action, roaring down the hall for a nurse to bring a wheelchair. When I saw my little Dell for the first time, he was yellow with jaundice and so tiny in the incubator. He stayed there two more weeks, coming home around my 17th birthday.

Glen and Lois

The first three months of Dell's life were rough with colic and he couldn't keep down any formula. He was literally starving to death, weighing just nine pounds at three months old. Lois was scared that he would get cold because he was so small, and kept the apartment heat at a suffocating level, causing heat blisters to form on Dell's tiny arms and legs.

The doctor visited Lois and Dell at the apartment and he scolded her for keeping the baby wrapped too tightly and the heat so high. He wouldn't listen to Lois' tales of the baby vomiting, being malnourished, or having colic. Even at seventeen years old, Lois knew the doctor was wrong. After she kept pressuring him for a solution, he told Lois to put Dell on plain old cow's milk, throw the formula out, and continue to love him as she did.

This time brought Glen and Lois closer to each other. Glen was touched by the hours of walking and rocking that Lois put in with Dell. When Lois' nerves were shot and tears spent, Glen took over with patience.

The small family was glad to finally get out of their apartment and move into half of a house until Dell was eighteen months old. Then Kennecott Cooper went on strike again, and Glen was out of work. The family returned to Glen's mother's house in Bluffdale. During the nine months of the strike, Lois and Glen never saw the financial support or the groceries promised, by the Union, to the men who walked out. Glen loaded trucks long enough to collect two paychecks, until the company found out he was a Kennecott striker. The family survived from their vegetable garden and family donations.

Lois spent some of this time learning to drive and getting her driver's license. She was embarrassed to death when Glen had to sign for her driver's permit. Here she was, married and rearing a child, but couldn't get a license on her own.

Lois was also pregnant again and the doctor put her on paregoric and bed rest every other week because of cramping, bleeding, and nausea. Lois discovered that the one contributing factor to the difficult pregnancies was another incompatibility of blood. Her blood type was O-, while Glen's turned out to be a rare AB+. Glen pitched in with the housework and cooking while Lois was in bed.

While she was pregnant, Lois' mind drifted back often to the earlier years of sexual molestation and pain, and sometimes she shook with fear for her baby.

After nine months, the strike ended. The wages helped Lois and Glen find a home in Kearns, Utah for which they paid $5000 in 1955. The young couple took great care to make this first home special. Glen built a mahogany china cabinet with glass doors for his wife. He put in a flagstone walk and a short, stone, wall in the back as well as grass in the yard. They were happy together with their small family.

Lois' brother Marv got out of prison and came to live with the family. Lois drove him to and from his work at the Lark Mine. Marv bought a set of bunk beds to put in the bedroom that he shared with Dell. It was only later that Lois found out that Marv had forged Glen's name on a contract that he signed with the Paris Furniture Store in Kearns.

Kennecott went on strike a second time, leaving Glen unemployed and with no money for house payments. With regret, Lois moved the family into an apartment on Draper Street. They had been married three years when Lois' mother came back into town. She brought her husband, Ray Ballard, to visit Lois and Glen and to see her grandson. Maybe she wanted to know that Lois' life had turned out all right or perhaps to ease her own guilt at leaving her younger daughter to the child welfare system. Lois was not to see Raymond again.

Lois and Glen's second child was born on October 12, 1956. They named me Debbie. Against the doctor's suggestions to not get pregnant again, Glen and Lois' third child, Karen, came into the world in December of 1958. Shortly thereafter, Glen moved the family to Riverside, California, to find work. From Riverside, the family lived all over Southern California in the following years.

Several times, the family was close to being evicted or there wasn't any money. Most of the jobs Glen took were construction based. So he just moved from one construction job to another looking for something stable, but he could never find a long-term job.

Lois had another violent miscarriage about nineteen months after Karen was born. She hadn't even known that she was pregnant. When partying and dancing with family members at a bar into the early morning hours, she went to bed exhausted. When she walked into the bathroom the next morning, Lois was shocked as she watched her body hemorrhaging blood. Returning to bed, she saw that her sheets were also soaked red. Lois did not remember the ambulance ride that brought her to the hospital emergency room. Rushing her directly to the operating table, the surgeon performed a D & C. Lois had to lie still for several hours afterward to prevent further bleeding. She received transfusions to compensate for the blood loss and shock to her body. With no insurance, the doctor sent Lois home for three weeks of bed rest.

Lois' mother came to stay with them to help out and get to know her granddaughters and grandson. This time together for Lois and her mother was healing for both of them. Never again would they

Lois and Bessie

be apart. Lois stayed close to her mom when she could and often traveled to Long Beach for visits. Lois' mom lived there alone, long divorced from Raymond Ballard. Lois learned to trust her mom in a way she had never been able as a child. She and her three children would spend weekends together with their grandma.

Debbie was four when she came down with the mumps. Lois, frantic that the other children would also get sick, called her mom to see if she would take Debbie for the couple of weeks that she would be contagious. The time with her grandmother had a lasting impression on Debbie—Grandma washing her long hair at night and coloring with her on the living room floor; Grandma making a formal dinner every night for the two of them to share; Debbie refusing to eat her peas until it was a point of contention for Grandma B.

When the two weeks was nearly up, Grandma asked Debbie if she liked her long hair that hung well past her knees.

"I hate it, Grandma. It's hot and hard to comb."

"Do you want me to cut it for you?"

"Oh yes, but won't Dad be mad?"

"Of course not, dear."

Debbie knew very well that her Dad would be angry, but she didn't care. Grandma Ballard cut Debbie's hair up to her ears. Glen and Lois almost fainted when they came to pick up their daughter the next morning.

Glen had to restrain himself from screaming at Grandma B. while Lois reminded him not to yell at her because she was too fragile. After settling down, Glen made his position clear: "If you want to see your granddaughter and remain friends, never cut Debbie's hair again."

While Glen may have been angry with Grandma B. for overstepping her bounds, the time that Debbie spent with her those few weeks created a strong and lasting bond between grandmother and granddaughter.

Grandma Ballard also had the most elegant tea parties with Lois and her girls. She would lay out one of her many teapots and good china cups from the hutch. The girls would sit at the kitchen table together telling stories and learning manners.

There were many lovely trips to Grandma's house to sort through her buckets of buttons and listen to her fascinating stories. Lois finally had her mother back. She invited Grandma B. to come stay for Christmas in 1961 when Debbie was five.

Lois and the children made candy with Grandma B. and sang songs and told stories. Grandma B. taught the children how to make presents with things they found. She also made sure they said their prayers every night.

This time was fun for the whole family and it seemed to be a good omen for times to come. Glen was working steadily for a big company, and Lois was working full time at the local newspaper. There wasn't a lot of money but the house payment was made, and the family had food and other necessities.

Yet, while Lois' relationship with her mother was healing, she and Glen started to have problems. Lois was working full time and on numerous occasions she didn't come home from work at all. She was angry all the time and never said much of anything except to yell at everyone. Then the day of the fishing trip came.

Glen took his children for a weekend trip to Lake Ellsinore when Lois was working all weekend and was unable to go. When they arrived at the lake Glen realized he had left his tackle box sitting in the driveway, so he gathered up Debbie and Karen and told Dell to stay put with his friends. It was a short drive back to the house and Glen knew the boys were old enough to stay out of trouble until he returned.

When they arrived at the house, Glen noticed that Lois was leaving and tried to flag her down. Lois kept going so Glen followed her and watched her pull into a local motel parking lot.

He was confused. *What was she doing?* Glen parked in the corner of the lot and watched as Lois got out of her car, walked over to an older man and embraced him. They went into a motel room together.

Dumbfounded and with children in the car, Glen sat there for what seemed like eternity to Debbie. Finally he pulled up in front of the room, told the girls not to move, got out of the car, and walked to the motel room. Glen stood in front of the door mustering up the courage to knock. He did knock, quite deliberately and with resolution.

Debbie peered through the car window as the old man opened the door and her father pushed his way into the room. Within seconds, Glen walked out, followed by a crying and screaming Lois.

Glen walked over to the car, opened the door without saying a word, got in and drove off. He drove to the house again, picked up his tackle box, and returned to the lake with the girls.

Glen went over to where Debbie was sitting on the beach and joined her on the sandy shore. While Karen was still in the car sleeping, Glen and Debbie sat in silence, staring at the water. Glen poured a cup of hot coffee from his thermos and took a sip, and then he started to cry. Debbie sat in silence holding her father's hand.

5

HISTORY REPEATS ITSELF
1966–1974

Life is like a game of cards. The hand that is dealt you represents determinism; the way you play it is free will.—Jawaharal Nehru

J sat next to my mom in church, like I did most Sundays. It was hard to sit still and my mind wandered to the beautiful weather outside. When the choir began to sing, I snapped to attention. This was always my favorite part of the worship service; when the people started singing, I could hear the angels join in. I wanted to know if Mom could hear them, too.

"Do you hear them now?" I looked up and asked her.

"Be quiet!" Not the response I was looking for.

"Mom, they're singing. Can't you hear the angels?" I asked a bit too loudly, ignoring her command to remain silent. I knew I was supposed to be quiet in church, but this was too important. I had to know if she heard them, because their music was so harmonious and beautiful.

Mom was clearly annoyed with me for asking her again, but there was more to that look. I saw anger mixed with fear in her eyes.

"Don't ever say that out loud. You'll get in trouble for that."

Reluctantly, I decided that from that point on, I had better enjoy the angelic music by myself.

Being raped by my uncle continued to haunt me, but I still didn't tell anyone. I couldn't. What would I say? How could a ten –year old put the whole ugly mess into words? And I was still afraid that no one would ever believe me.

My uncle would just deny it, and I thought they'd believe him and not me. I buried it deep inside of me, figuring that if I just kept trying to forget it ever happened, I'd be fine.

But the memory of the trauma haunted my sleep and even my waking hours. I became adept at pushing the memory deeper and deeper into my ocean of forgetfulness. When the wave of memory would surface again, I'd push it back. It seemed an unending and unnerving cycle of pain.

Lois, Debbie, and siblings

One night when I was ten years old, when I was startled awake in the middle of the night by a noise. Did I hear mumbling? Some sort of sound was coming from the living room. Mom was at work and everybody else should have been asleep. Wide-awake now, I crept to the living room to see what was going on. There I found Dad and the neighbor lady, both of them completely naked.

I couldn't believe what I was seeing. I just stared at my dad, thinking, *Jeez, how could you be doing this?*

There was no explanation or apology from him, just a plea. "Don't tell your mother," he said. "Debbie, promise me you won't tell your mother. Please?"

"All right." I stormed back to my room and cried tears of hurt and confusion.

The next morning, I couldn't wait to reveal my secret. I was so angry with my dad for ruining the image that I had of him that I blurted it out to Mom over breakfast. Mom was supposed to be the "bad guy," not Dad. Mom was the one who always yelled at me and criticized everything I did. She was the one always cheating on my dad, having her affairs. In my eyes, Dad had always been the "good guy." Not anymore.

Dad looked at me as though I had just stabbed him in the back but I didn't care. I just wanted to hurt him the way he had hurt me. However, I didn't expect his next action. He got up and left. He disappeared with that horrid woman. My brother and sister—I was the middle child—blamed me, hating me for "driving him away." They started calling me "Big Mouth Bass," my awful nickname from that point on. Mom refused to talk to me the whole time Dad was gone. I just hid in my room. Four days later, Dad finally came back.

Dear God, Daddy left and it's my fault. I'm sorry. I didn't mean to tell, it just slipped out. I was so mad at them. I hate them both!

That's when I learned that the cheating was mutual. I came to realize that Mom and Dad had always cheated on each other.

Mom's affairs were no secret to me, or to anyone in the family for that matter.

More than once, Dad brought me along when he followed her to hotels. I sat in the car and waited while he walked into the room and dragged her out. I saw the man she was sleeping with and he looked like he was in his seventies.

Dear God, we are following Mom and she is with some old man. If she's going to be doing this, why doesn't she at least pick someone young and cute? I hate her. She's ruining everything.

I didn't understand her behavior. I didn't like it, either. The truth was, Mom was looking for love and, in a very twisted way, searching for a father. Dad was trying to hurt her the way she hurt him. It was a matter of getting even. I even heard him tell her, "Well, if you're gonna do it, so am I. I'll go find somebody to have an affair with."

He did. Mom even made it easy for him by setting him up for affairs. What the hell was she doing, trying to relieve her own sense of guilt? She even brought a woman into the house to live with us. She and her daughter stayed in our home for almost a year. I hated her and her brat daughter. We never had much of anything and this brat got whatever she asked for. New dresses . . . oh, how I always wanted a new dress for school, but I only got my cousins' hand me downs.

Mom worked nights, so this woman befriended my father and, of course, they had an affair, right there with all of us kids around.

I was far beyond being sick of my parents' fighting and affairs. I hated both of them so much for what they were doing to each other, and to me and my siblings. Why did they have to fight all the time? It drove me crazy. I was sick of their shouting, threats, and insults. I spent most of my time hiding in my room, wishing for a better family, wishing I never had to come out of my room again.

Dear God, it's me again. Please could I have a happy family? When I grow up my kids will be happy. I will make cookies and read to them and be up in the morning and make breakfast and they will always have new clothes for school.

I wanted a normal life, not this. I wanted happy parents who loved each other and actually paid attention to their kids. I swore that when I got married some day, my kids would never have to listen to that kind of crap over and over again. Little did I know, I would end up outdoing my own parents.

Life in the city wasn't working out for us. My dad was in construction and, as long as I could remember, we had moved from one place to the next with Dad, following jobs. We were not in good shape financially, and we were losing our house yet again. For what seemed to me the hundredth time, we had to move.

I was thirteen when I met Joe. His little brother and I attended the same junior high school. From what I'd heard, Joe had been through a lot. His little sister had died at the age of five after tripping on the sidewalk and breaking her neck. Joe was just eight when that happened. His mother desperately wanted another baby girl to replace her lost daughter. After having one more boy, she became pregnant again and fell ill with the Hong Kong flu. It killed her and her unborn child. Joe was fifteen when he lost his mom.

Three months after his mom died, his father, an extremely rigid and controlling man, kicked him out of the house. He was out of control, not going to school and in trouble with the law. He spent two years living on the streets of Northern California, alone. His father finally let him come home after Joe begged and promised he would never get in trouble again. He was not allowed to go to the same school as his younger brother and he had to stay in the babies' room. His father was remarried now to a woman with four of her own children, all of them much younger than Joe. Joe spent all his free time doing chores and watching the babies.

At the same time, my dad took a job managing a farm and with so much work to do, Dad told Joe that he could work on the farm and live with our family.

That is how seventeen-year-old Joe came to stay with my family and cemented my future into foundations of turmoil.

Because his younger brother and I already were close friends, the three of us started hanging out together, despite our age differences. I liked being with Joe. He was a different, mysterious, older guy who paid attention to me. When I turned fourteen, I had my first sexual experience with Joe. A few more sexual encounters followed.

Dear God, it's me. I think I am in love. I met this boy and he is special. He treats me good and pays attention to me. Do you think he likes me? I hope he does. Bye for now, me.

My parents knew about us, but they didn't try to stop it. They were too busy with their own drama to pay enough attention to the trouble I was getting into. By the time I was fifteen I had discovered pot and become friends with drug dealers. I was completely out of control.

Because I would rather smoke pot and stay high all day than go to school, my mother put me in counseling. She knew something was terribly wrong. It was obvious. I was constantly getting into trouble.

I could tell that my counselor had figured out what had happened to me when I was younger. I was scared, and I didn't want to go back. Until now, I had kept the rape locked deep inside me where nobody could see. When she flat out asked me if I had been sexually abused, I couldn't hold back my tears. She knew. She convinced me that telling my parents was the right thing to do. I didn't want to tell them, but my counselor was firm. She said it would help.

A week later my parents were invited to counseling and with a lot of persuasion I told them what had happened. I told them what

my uncle had done to me—how he had robbed me of my innocence. My father started to cry. In my entire life I hadn't seen him
cry like that. He stood up, left the room without saying a word or
even looking at me, and disappeared for a week. *What happened?*
Where did he go? Did he hate me for telling him about this awful thing
that happened so long ago? Was it my fault? Even though Mom tried
to reassure me that Dad just needed some time, I didn't believe her.
It was one of the longest weeks of my life.

Hi God, my dad is gone again. And again it's my fault. I can't do any-
thing right. He hates me. I have done something horrible. I will take it
back if you send him home. Please God. Love, Me

It turned out that my father went to Utah to kill his brother. He
stalked him for a week, watching him go to and from work, waiting
for the right moment to shoot him. Thank God he convinced himself that this was not the answer. At the end of that week, he turned
around and came back home to us.

When Dad saw me, he immediately rushed over to hold me. We
both cried as he told me how sorry he was that this had happened.
For the first time in a very long time, I felt close to my father.

That image I once had of him was restored, at least partially.
Dad cared about me after all. I begged him to please never, ever
confront my uncle, and to never bring this up again until I was
ready to talk about it. He understood. He made me a promise and
he kept his word. He never brought it up again, honoring my need
for privacy on this matter. As far as I was concerned, that was the
end of it, except that I still was smoking pot all of the time and
never going to school. I did get a job though. I was cleaning apartments for Air Force guys down the street. This made things much
worse between my Mom and me. I was high all the time and hanging out with men ten years older than me.

Dad moved to Utah soon after he and Mom finally separated. He told me they needed some time apart and that he couldn't fight anymore. I hated him for leaving me with her. My brother and Joe followed my father, so it was Mom, my sister, and I.

I was fifteen when my mom insisted that I take my sister Karen to a weekend party with me. Mom's boyfriend was coming over and she wanted us both out of the house for the night. I promptly ditched Karen at the party, leaving her at the mercy of my drug friends who offered her pills. She overdosed and was transported to the nearest city with a major hospital.

It just so happened that my father, brother and Joe had come down for the weekend to take care of some things and Dad sent Joe to find me. He finally found me at about two in the morning and drove me down the mountain to where Karen was in the ER. My parents were both sitting by her bed when I entered the room. I was crying and walked over to her when a police officer came in and ordered me out of the room. He told me that my sister had nearly died because of me and ordered me to tell him exactly what took place at the party and who gave my sister the drugs. I was scared to death and felt like I had just totally failed at everything, including being a sister. My parents just stood there and didn't say a word.

I wanted to see my sister so I could hold her hand and tell her how sorry I was. I wanted to tell her how much I loved her and that I would never leave her alone again. But they wouldn't let me talk to her for two weeks after that night. I went to detention. I told the police everything they asked me. I named names and told them where to find the guys who gave my sister the drugs. When I finally returned home, my parents told me to stay away from my sister and I did. I retreated to my room and stayed there. Then the phone calls started, telling my Dad that if I testified I wouldn't live long enough to see the courtroom. They told my parents they would kill everyone in our family while we slept. They told them they would torture me after they killed my family and then kill me.

My dad finally had enough and told my mom to pack our things as we were all going to move to Utah. While we were away on one of our trips moving our belongings, the drug dealers broke into our home and destroyed it. They murdered my dog and her five-week-old puppies to stop me from testifying against them.

Dad decided that I would not testify and he called the detective and told him that we were moving and not to contact any of us again. That was it. We packed up and moved to Utah, away from the trouble I had found. I spent all my time with Joe from then on. In the midst of the chaos of my parents' cheating and fighting and me doing drugs, I figured that sticking with him was probably the best thing I could do for myself. I stayed right by his side, trying my hardest to become everything he expected me to be. I never did tell my sister how I felt that night or how sorry I was. I knew I had let everyone who loved me down, including myself. I couldn't even look in the mirror. That's when I learned to hate myself.

When I was sixteen, I became pregnant. Joe wasn't too happy about it, but he told me he'd marry me anyway because it was the right thing to do. We were married in 1973, and I thought it was the absolute best thing that had ever happened to me. I desperately wanted to get away from my parents' fighting and cheating on each other, away from the drugs and the dealers, and away from the memory of being raped by my uncle at the age of nine. All I wanted was to run away with the man of my dreams, have children, and live happily ever after.

Our first year of marriage went fairly well. I enjoyed being a mommy to our son, Shawn, and playing house. By the second year, though, it was a whole different story. That's when a peculiar side of Joe emerged, and living in hell began for me all over again.

6

UNDER HIS CONTROL
1974–1985

If you do not hope, you will not find what is beyond your hopes.
—St. Clement of Alexandria

*A*fter our wedding day, we moved into a tiny trailer on State Street in Salt Lake City. At seventeen and twenty, we were two kids on our own, with a baby on the way. We struggled with the newness of it all. As hard as we tried, we couldn't make it work on our own financially. So only five months after Joe and I married, we moved back in with my parents in Kearns.

> *Dear God, Hi it's me. How are you? As you know I am very happy. Thank you, God. I love being a wife. I will be the best ever. Thank you for answering my prayers. I can feel the baby growing. I'm kinda scared. What if I'm not good at being a Mom? Please tell Joe it's ok to be happy. Talk soon! Love, Me*

Joe was miserable living with my parents. I had mixed feelings about it, but a part of me was relieved to be living back home with Mom and Dad. I thought they could help me take care of the baby and I was smart enough to know that I needed the help. I really didn't know much about taking care of babies.

To my relief, giving birth to my firstborn was not difficult at all.

Labor went smoothly and before I knew it, I was cradling Shawn in my arms. What a heady experience for a teenager to be holding her own baby—exhilarating and terrifying at the same time.

My parents tried to give us well-meaning advice about the baby, our finances, and our marriage, but Joe shut them out. He didn't want to hear it from them, even if it was good advice. He refused to show Mom even an ounce of respect unless Dad was around, then he was different.

He used to shut himself in our bedroom, and distance himself from my family. It irked me that he expected me to stay shut in with him. He didn't need me by his side like that; he just wanted to control me.

I hated being cooped up and isolated from my parents, so I would go out to talk with them and clear my mind. Not that interacting with them was easy. On the one hand, I had no idea what to do with a newborn, and I expected too much help from my mom. On the other hand, my parents didn't know how to handle their married teen daughter with a baby! Between Joe, my parents, and me, there was plenty of friction.

Despite the tension, I *needed* my parents' help, needed to get out of that bedroom and connect with someone other than my husband. But Joe wouldn't hear of it. Not five minutes would pass until he would come to our bedroom door, glaring, cursing, and yelling at me to return to our room. I felt humiliated.

On the up side, I spent hours in our bedroom bonding with Shawn. He was a beautiful baby. I couldn't believe that this tiny little person was mine. I felt woefully unprepared to be a mom, and my feelings matched the reality of the situation. But I also thanked God for the miracle of this precious little baby. I was content to simply hold Shawn for long stretches at a time and gaze at his precious little face.

Hi God, it's me. The baby is so little and warm, I love to hold him. Why doesn't Joe like to hold him? I don't understand him. Thank you for Shawn, I love him. Please make Joe love him and Thank you again God. Love, Debbie

Joe didn't like me spending so much time with Shawn, holding him for hours. He accused me of spoiling him. I argued with him, explaining that babies needed to be held and loved. That's when Joe lost his temper and grabbed me by the throat. He looked at me in a way that frightened me. He told me never to argue with him again. I felt the tears coming and tried to hold them back. This wasn't the first angry outburst of his—there were a lot of them. I started being very cautious around him with the baby. When he was home I wouldn't cradle my child in my arms as much as I wanted to.

Once Mom and I were together late in the evening while Shawn slept. Nobody else was around. Mom's voice broke the silence.

"Do you still hear voices?" she asked.

I couldn't believe it. After all these years, she *still* had it wrong. I wasn't hearing voices! I told her so, quite emphatically. I again explained that I heard angelic music that filled me with a sense of peace I couldn't find anyplace else.

"Why can't you just allow me this?" I snapped at her. Nothing had changed. She tried to convince me that this was a bad thing and that I should never tell anyone about them. Exasperated, I got up and went to check on the baby.

When Shawn turned three months old, Joe finally couldn't take living with my parents any longer. We moved into an apartment in West Jordan. Thus began our life together as an independent family unit of mommy, daddy, and baby. Away from my parents, life became a little less tense, but not easier.

Surprisingly, Joe and I stayed together. I guess that says a lot about our stamina. Joe insisted that I be a stay-at-home mom. Not so much for Shawn's benefit, but because if I stayed at home, Joe would have more control over my life. He wanted to make sure that I had absolutely no outside contact whatsoever—which I didn't. With no phone and no car, I was alone except for Shawn.

I didn't care because I was happy at home with my baby. As a child, I had longed for a perfect home, and now I carried that vision over into my marriage. I tried to create that—happy parents, happy little family, good mommy. I even baked my own bread, and did everything I felt a good homemaker would do.

Unfortunately, that vision of a happy family didn't exactly play out the way I wanted it to. Just like my parents did, Joe and I argued. He liked to criticize me and make me feel like I couldn't do anything right in his eyes. I looked forward to evenings when Joe would go to the bar with his buddies and I could be alone with Shawn. It was peaceful.

However, controlling and absent from my life, Joe was a very good provider. As a dry waller, he earned a decent living. Even when we struggled to make ends meet, there was enough to eat, so at least we never went hungry. But I was starting to feel a different kind of hunger deep in my soul. I was lonely and needed to see my dad. I missed him and I desperately needed him in my life.

Joe would leave home for two or three weeks at a time to work in Nevada, which was booming with new construction. He used the excuse of having to find work. The deep-down real truth, though, was that he was running away from Shawn and me. He didn't want to feel tied down, and his response was to disappear every so often. I was scared to be left alone with the baby in that apartment and I could feel my heart breaking.

Joe would send enough money to pay the rent and buy groceries, but nothing more. He had it figured down to the last penny and I never had any extra money. I felt so very alone. Even when he was there with me, I was alone.

Hi God, why doesn't he care? Why is he running away? He has his own private life away from Shawn and me. He values his friends and his life away from home more than he values being a husband and dad. Not only is he distant from me, he is also distant from the baby. He doesn't want to get too close. How could he not love Shawn or me? What's wrong with him? Doesn't he know he is hurting me? What did I do? God please tell me and I will fix it. Me

Joe was often cruel to his own son. Spankings were abusive and when Shawn would fuss or cry too much, Joe would beat his butt and throw him into his crib. He was always mean and violent with Shawn, just like his own father had been with him. When I dared intervene he would scream at me, warning me to stay out of it.

Hi God. I'm pregnant!

Maybe bringing another child into the picture wasn't a good idea, but regardless of that, I became pregnant again. Just as with the first pregnancy, Joe wasn't happy about it. At twenty-two, he wasn't ready for a growing family. Emotionally, he couldn't handle it.

He had resented me for years for getting pregnant with Shawn and forcing him into marriage and now, to my surprise, I was starting to resent him, too. He was gone for an entire month near the end of my second pregnancy. I was angry and I hated him for leaving me alone while I was pregnant. It was the first time I felt hatred toward him. I did, however, get a phone in the apartment. I explained to Joe that if he was leaving for very long I might go into labor and I had to be able to call Dad if I needed him to come and get me. And I did—every day, asking Dad to come and get Shawn and me. I spent all afternoon with my parents, catching up on everything we missed. Mom and Dad loved being able to spend time with their grandson. I didn't want Joe to come home because I was happy with him gone. Shawn and I spent as much time as we wanted at my parents' house and when we were home we had fun playing and reading stories. There was no yelling and no name-calling. No one called me stupid and no one interfered with me loving my little boy. Three and a half weeks after Joe had left he returned and life was hell again for a while. Joe made sure I knew how angry he was about me spending so much time at my parents'. Eventually he regained his control over us and everything was a little calmer for a while.

With the baby due any day, we moved out of the apartment and into a trailer we bought. I was ecstatic because we moved across the street from my parents. I stopped being scared of being alone. My dad was right across the street, and I finally felt safe again. Joe found the trailer through a friend of his and he knew it was close to my parents. When he found out it was across the street he almost backed out but it was such a good deal he took it. Life was easier there, as I had Dad close to me, watching us all the time.

My second delivery was as trouble-free as my first. I gave birth to a pretty little girl, and we named her Wendy. At twenty, I had a three-year-old son, a newborn daughter, and a mostly absentee husband.

Joe threw himself into working and partying with his friends. When we were first married, he would leave me home for several hours to go out drinking with his friends. Now, he would be gone all night. But I had a saving grace—Mom and Dad across the street from me.

Every day, I took the kids with me to visit my parents after they came home from work. They were terrific grandparents to Shawn and Wendy, and I was glad to have someone to talk to.

Dad loved playing Grandpa and my kids enjoyed hearing him tell all kinds of wild, make-believe stories. Dad would get on all fours and play with them right at their level. It was a hoot. He gave them lots of hugs and my children knew that their Grandpa would always be there for them.

The kids were always well behaved when their father was around. But they knew that around *my* father they could be themselves. Dad quickly became Shawn's role model and self-esteem booster. Joe was verbally abusive with Shawn from the time he was a baby, so being with Grandpa meant that he could be a child and not live in fear of doing the wrong thing.

Dad intervened for my kids when he could. When Joe called Shawn a crybaby for crying, my dad stepped in. He told Shawn, "Never be ashamed of crying. Never. To be able to cry in public is a sign of strength."

Dad corrected a lot of the mean things that Joe said to Shawn. He was a pillar of strength my son could lean on. Joe only called Shawn stupid once in front of my father. After that he would save his words until my father was not around. Joe always knew better than go against Dad. There was a respect there that I had never seen Joe show anyone else.

Mom and I still had our issues. My resentment toward Joe was just emerging, but my resentment toward my Mom had been brewing for years. Like Joe, she worked a lot. She dedicated herself to helping foster children because she herself had once been a foster child. Maybe I should have been proud of her for what she did, but because I'd felt neglected as a child, I was still harboring anger.

She didn't have time for me, I'd find myself thinking. She liked those kids better than she had ever liked me. She would bring them home for the holidays and I hated all of them and I hated her for doing it.

Then something happened that brought me closer to my mother. Her mother, my grandmother, came to live with them. She was getting up in years and was becoming forgetful, almost senile. Mom had her move in with them so they could take care of her. Her plan was for my grandmother to live there for the rest of her life. That's what she wanted.

I was so happy to have Grandma Ballard nearby! She was a beautiful light in my life. Every day at noon, I went across the street and walked Grandma B. to my house where we had lunch together. Then she watched her soap operas while we talked and reminisced. Grandma B. loved to hold Wendy, gently rocking her back and forth. She told me that I should be thankful for my husband and glad that he didn't beat me or make me go hungry. This was my grandma's belief and this was how she was taught. Women kept their place and did as they were told. When I told her that I wanted to go back to school and learn, she smiled at me and said, "Whatever for my dear? Aren't you well taken care of?"

I will never forget how that made me feel. I thought I was ungrateful for being so angry about the way Joe always made me feel so stupid. I felt *bad* that I could never seem to make him happy. I decided that I would work harder at trying to be smart and sexy. I knew then that it was my fault my marriage was not working. I was going to fix it! I loved talking to Grandma B. because she was so understanding and always gave me good advice to keep working on my marriage. She never told me to leave Joe because he was not good for me, the way my mom did. I'd never been happier.

That happy time was short-lived. Six months after Grandma moved in with my parents, three of my mother's older siblings came, took her away, and put her in a nursing home. The worst part was that they refused to tell Mom where Grandma was.

I was there when they came and took her. One was an uncle to whom I'd always felt especially close. Seeing him like this was an absolute shock for me. I had never seen him so mean and hateful before. He even insulted my father in front of me. It was a horrible episode.

Mom's siblings did this because they hated her and they hated their mother. They didn't want my grandmother to have a happy ending. Grandmother spent the rest of her life hidden away in a nursing home. It took my mom a year and half to finally find her in California near where Betty lived. One day Mom came home from work and told Dad she was going to find her mother. She packed the car, called a friend to go with her and she was off. I remember Dad asking how Mom was going to find her; she told him that she would pray about it.

When Mom got to the area where she thought Grandma might be staying, she checked every nursing home within a ten-mile radius and found nothing. The second and third day went by with no results. She was losing hope and pulled to the side of the road and that was when she prayed. When she stopped crying, she looked up and saw the church across the street from where she was parked. Mom got out of her car and went to ask at the church and see if they knew of a nursing home that she might have missed. She walked in and the pastor met her at the door. He asked her if there was something he could help her with and she told him her story. He reassured her that she had visited all of the nursing homes in the area. Mom was devastated ready to give up and go home. When she turned to walk out, the pastor asked her what grandma looked like. After Mom described her to him he told Mom there was a woman that fit the description that he would visit and read to. He told Mom where she was and asked her to check back; he was certain it was Grandma.

Mom went back to that nursing home and when they again told her that Grandma B. wasn't there, Mom decided to go out through the back door. She walked down the hall and heard a woman crying and she knew it was Grandma. The nursing home had been given strict orders to tell anyone that came in looking for my grandma that she wasn't there. Mom and Grandma were so happy to be reunited, but only a week later, Grandma passed away.

Grandma's death almost killed Mom. This wasn't how she had pictured her mother's final years. She was devastated and angry with her siblings for their cruelty. I, too, was angry with Mom's side of the family.

I felt Mom's pain. The whole event was so unfair and so pointless. For the first time in a long time, my heart went out to my Mom.

Little Wendy turned eighteen months old and with the kids growing so quickly, Joe decided it was time to move up in the world. We sold our trailer and were able to make enough money for a down payment on our first house.

I loved that house in Magna. My husband helped build it and I had the fun part—picking out the carpet, the cabinets, the tile, the curtains, and everything inside within our financial limitations. This was my dream house and fixing it up was one of my happiest moments.

Lasting happiness, however, continued to escape us. Joe still had his party friends. They stayed out all night and he was almost never home. He was gone until two or three in the morning and I rarely ever saw him. I clung to what Grandma had told me about being a good wife and just kept trying harder to please him.

Joe was drunk most of the time. He had a true alcohol addiction and it made him angry. Somehow, it never interfered with his work. But it sure interfered with what little family life we had.

One afternoon, I received a disturbing and anonymous letter in the mail. Whoever wrote it wanted to warn me that I might have contracted a venereal disease from my husband. *What? So this is what he'd been doing away from me! How many people had he slept with all these years?* When I confronted Joe with the letter he flipped out. Instead of allowing me my justifiable anger, *he* got angry. He insisted the letter was a mistake, a practical joke. Even though I knew better, I didn't want to face the truth, so I gave him the benefit of the doubt. And besides, that is what a good wife would do.

We started playing a stupid game where he pretended he wasn't cheating on me, and I pretended to believe him. I chose to turn a blind eye on his carousing with women. Maybe I did that because I couldn't handle any more than what I was dealing with in my life already. His drunken bouts at home were mean and verbally abusive. He called me awful names if I didn't do exactly what he wanted in the bedroom. "You can't even make me happy," he would scream at me. "You do the same thing over and over again. Why don't you think of something new and creative so I'm not bored with you?"

My self-esteem was shot.

Joe would constantly tell me how stupid I was in front of the kids. And the kids were always there. "Your mother doesn't know anything," he would tell our children. "Don't listen to her. She has no clue what she's doing. She's stupid." Whenever the kids acted up, I didn't bother to discipline them in front of him. I knew Joe would just yell at me for "doing it all wrong."

I began to see more clearly the addictive side of Joe's personality. He could hide it well. When he had important paperwork to do at home, he wouldn't drink. He had some level of discipline in him when he wanted to, but more and more, Joe seemed to succumb to his addictions. When it wasn't alcohol, it was sex, and when it wasn't sex, it was smoking. There was always something.

If there was one love in his life, it was our young Wendy. He never, ever abused her. He loved her dearly and protected her, telling her that she was Daddy's little girl. When Shawn got carried away teasing Wendy, he would encounter severe discipline from his dad—the humiliation, name calling and abrupt smacks upside the head when he didn't expect it.

Three years after we moved into my dream house, we lost it. The construction industry took a turn for the worse in the early 1980s, and Joe had a hard time finding and keeping jobs. We went bankrupt, and our home was repossessed. We had lost our beautiful home and moved into a dumpy apartment.

Because construction jobs were so hard to find in Utah, Joe went looking for work in Wyoming. He spent a year and a half there, coming home to the kids and me every three weeks. When he worked in Wyoming, he became heavily involved in using drugs, selling drugs, and sleeping with prostitutes.

When he came home, he would bring scary people with him. They were selling drugs out of our apartment with him. I was afraid of them and afraid for my children.

I was so scared and lonely that I came dangerously close to stooping to Joe's level of behavior. I became friends with a guy Joe knew. He seemed like a really nice guy, and I appreciated that, unlike my husband, he treated me respectfully. We became close emotionally, and this led to a physical attraction.

I almost had a full-blown affair with him. I went as far as getting undressed and climbing into bed with him when an alarm went off in my head. *What was I doing?* I got scared and left before I had sex with him. What scared me was the person I'd become. I felt so ashamed that I was becoming just like Joe, or worse, just like my mother.

Life continued to get only worse with Joe. The drugs and the alcohol were making him act crazier. He got meaner and meaner and soon nothing was ever good enough for him. He wanted more and more sex. Whenever I wasn't willing to have sex with him, he would go find prostitutes and former girlfriends in Nevada and California who were more than willing to sleep with him.

In front of the kids, he treated me even worse than before. After I came back from the grocery store, he would grab the receipt and check every item. When I bought crayons and a coloring book for the kids, he gave me a three-hour-long rambling lecture that went something like this: "You idiot! You know we don't have any money. What the hell is wrong with you?" He went on and on in front of the kids for three hours about how stupid I was, how I couldn't handle anything, not even grocery shopping.

I had to get out of that horrible environment. It was making me sick. With Shawn in first grade and Wendy now three years old, I got my first job. Leaving Wendy with a sitter, I went to work at a place called Ames Taping Tools where I repaired tools. I enjoyed the freedom, but Joe kept a close eye on me. I repaired tools that he used for his trade, so he pretty much knew everybody who went in and out of the store. I didn't know it at the time, but Joe even had an affair with the woman I worked for.

I was out in the "real world," and Joe was scared. He was losing his tight grip on me, so he resorted to more name calling, more belittling, more mind games and money control. If I wanted to do something on my own, I had to sneak out to do it.

I had worked at Ames Taping Tools for nearly a year when my daughter gave me the scare of my life. Still three years old—nearly four now—Wendy ran away from the babysitter's house. She walked by herself along a busy highway for six miles to our home. That absolutely terrified me.

I knew the babysitter was a horrible woman, but Joe had insisted she was fine. *How could she be fine if my young daughter ran away from her?* That sent a strong signal that something was very wrong at the sitter's house. I was angry with Joe for making me leave her there. I was angry with myself for listening to him.

I told Dad that I was going to quit my job to stay home with the kids and he offered to take them for me until he went back to work and I finally had to quit. I became a stay-at-home mom again until Wendy started school.

When both of my kids were finally in school, I was bored being home all day and went looking for another job. I checked the paper and found a "Help Wanted" ad for proofreaders for a check-printing company. I went, applied, and got the job! It was a good feeling to know that I did this on my own.

I was gaining greater independence and self-worth through my job, but my personal life was still a mess. I struggled to make my life better, to find happiness somewhere. Maybe another baby was the answer.

In 1985, little Katy was born. By then, Wendy was eight and Shawn was eleven. Joe, as usual, wasn't happy about it.

7

A WAKE-UP CALL
1985–1986

"The remarkable thing we have is a choice every day regarding the attitude we will embrace for that day. We cannot change our past. We cannot change the fact that people will act in a certain way. We cannot change the inevitable. The only thing we can do is play on the one string we have, and that is our attitude."—Charles Swindoll

Throughout my pregnancy with Katy, Joe treated me with contempt. "You're on your own with this one," he told me bitterly again and again. "Don't talk to me about anything."

What a joke. I was already on my own.

Getting pregnant with Katy was my choice. I wanted her even though I knew serious repercussions would follow. Joe was so angry with me. He didn't want the two children we had, let alone another one.

The immediate punishment came in the form of Joe's escalating rudeness and cruel words. I endured his verbal abuse throughout my entire pregnancy and tried my best to block it out. I didn't care what he said. I had my job. I had Shawn and Wendy. And I had Katy growing and tumbling inside me.

Katy was born on July 17th 1985, and I took off a month from work to stay home with her. She was absolutely precious. Just like with my first two, I couldn't get enough of holding her in my arms and staring at her sweet little face. I was so happy. This time, though, I couldn't be an at-home mommy for her and I had to go back to work.

With Wendy and Shawn in school, I left Katy with a babysitter and went back to work. I tried to juggle it all, but the guilt I felt about leaving Katy with someone else was torturous. I cried every day when I left her and it was hard on both of us. Still so young, she was already being shuttled from one babysitter to the next.

I had trouble finding a good babysitter or daycare for Katy. It was important to me that Katy was safe. But it seemed each babysitter was worse than the next—not feeding or changing her. After Katy fell down the stairs in a horrific accident with the last babysitter, I decided to move to daycare.

Like with the babysitters, I had several problems until finally, I found a good center for Katy.

In addition to working, I started taking classes at the Salt Lake Community College in pre-press paste up, graphics and layout, and on running a five-color press. I then took business and financial classes. The experience was liberating. Away from home, I felt my self-esteem grow and relished learning new things. Away from Joe's abuse, and discovering life on my own for the first time, I finally felt like a real person.

The only downside was that I still felt like a terrible mom for being away from Katy. I had wanted her so badly, and now that she was here, I spent too much time at work and school. I felt that she wasn't getting the attention she needed from me because I was working fourteen to sixteen hour days and tried to cram in as much school as I could. Although the kids spent evenings with Grandma and Grandpa when I went to class, the guilt was still there for being absent in their lives. Dad and Mom filled the gap in the evenings and I narrowed my classes down to twice a week.

I began to feel the walls crashing in around me. My children weren't getting the love and attention they needed—especially the baby.

Katy was a sick child. She had ear infections constantly as well as other problems. She was also emotionally starved with me gone so much, and mediocre to awful caregivers. I missed many hours of work coming home early to get Katy from the sitter and take her to the doctor's office or to the drugstore for medicine. I dropped out of school and desperately tried to keep my job.

My boss was angry about the many hours away from the office and told me I had to get my priorities straight. I was perpetually torn between wanting to take good care of Katy and trying to hang on to my job. I sent Shawn and Wendy to the neighbors and tried to free myself from running, picking them up and dropping them off. It was my neighbor Gail's request that our kids play together on weekends and she knew how much time I spent going back and forth. It made it easier that they were right next door so I could get Katy and go straight home to spend time with them. My dad missed them but he understood and came to see them on weekends when he could.

My children were my priority, but my job was my lifeline. It gave me the strength to endure Joe's growing abuse. His sexual addictions became more intense and vicious, as did his desire to control me. I was finally out in the world, working and studying, meeting people, and making my own money. There was nothing he could do about that so he took it out on me in the bedroom. It became more and more unbearable. I hated him more and more every day.

Hi God, I don't know what to do. I'm so confused. I hate my life and I hate Joe. I hate the way he treats me like a piece of meat. I hate myself for not stopping him. Why doesn't he love me? God, what's wrong with me? Me

Why didn't I leave Joe? I was starving for him to love me and, as sick as it sounds, I desperately wanted my marriage to work.

Even though he broke my heart on a daily basis, in countless ways, I still believed that the romantic love myth could save our marriage. Behind Joe's back, I went to counselors, hoping they had the right formula or a key that I could use to turn our marriage around. *There's got to be a way to make it work,* I convinced myself.

With me working, our financial situation quickly improved. We finally had enough money to pay the bills, live without constantly worrying about finances, and have a little extra to put away in a savings account. With one area of our life improving, I had great hopes that the other areas would get better, too. I had dreams of owning our own home again someday and that day came, to my surprise.

My father-in-law, Joe's father, was very intimidating. He demanded that everyone treat him as if he was more important or more worthy than anyone else could ever be. He was very abusive to Joe as a child and belittled him constantly. Joe could never do anything right as far as Spencer was concerned, and that lead to physical abuse as well.

Even though he treated me differently, almost kindly, I had never had a lot of respect for Joe's father. You can't respect someone you are afraid of. I didn't have daily contact with him, but I did see him being even meaner and more controlling than Joe. So it surprised me immensely when he offered to put a down payment on a house for us so we could try to have our own home again. While I was still afraid of him, I appreciated his gesture immensely.

It truly was a big deal. Sure, we had to pay that down payment back, but it was a chance for us to have a new beginning. Joe and I accepted his dad's offer, found a house, and moved into our new home. It was an older house that needed a few repairs here and there, but it was ours. With help from my paychecks and Joe's work going well we were able to make our house payments. We used our tax write-off for the house to eventually repay the loan.

Despite my counseling sessions and our new start, our home life did not get better. In fact, it continued to deteriorate as Joe's abuse escalated. Thanks to my job and my classes, I was getting stronger, and I sensed that Joe feared that strength. So he shifted his focus to our son, Shawn, becoming more violent with him.

Joe started to smack Shawn around much more than he ever had. When I tried to stop it, Joe would tell me to stay out of it or he would make sure I was sorry–telling me what an idiot I was and how I was a horrible mother. He said that if I was smart, and knew how to raise a boy in to a man, he wouldn't have to beat Shawn. All of us learned to walk on eggshells, doing everything in our power to keep the peace and avoid disturbing the tentative balance at home. Even when the fear of physical abuse was present, we also had to endure an endless stream of verbal cruelty.

Far too often, Joe sat all of us down at the kitchen table and lectured us on how stupid and useless we were. It got to the point where I started to play a game with the children behind Joe's back, just to break the awful tension we felt. I smiled at Shawn and the girls, making faces whenever my husband wasn't looking. I silently mimicked him, or else I pretended to say, "Blah, blah, blah . . . " Anything to let my kids know they were all right and these were just a bunch of lies that didn't mean anything. It was my way of saying to them, "Hang in there, it's almost over. Any minute now he'll shut up and we can get up and leave. Just agree with him!"

Joe's control over Shawn made him feel totally worthless as a son. The long-term damage to my son's ego was so severe that I could never make it better. By the time my son was in the sixth grade, the control had become overpowering and the abuse was psychologically detrimental. Joe did everything he could to convince Shawn that he was absolutely stupid and worthless, and that he needed to rely on his dad for everything.

Despite efforts from my father and me to rebuild my son's esteem, the damage was done. Shawn believed that he couldn't do a thing right without his dad. He closed up and stopped sharing with me completely. His grandpa could still talk to him, but Shawn would shrug him off if any positive comments were made.

Shawn would tell my dad how stupid he was and he couldn't

do anything right. Shawn asked Dad if he could move in with him and Grandma if he tried not to be too stupid. This broke my father's heart to hear and he just wanted to take Shawn and run. He knew that wasn't possible so he kept showing up in Shawn's life for his baseball games, school programs and anything else he could support. He was the same with Wendy, always showing up at school programs and soccer games. Joe was never there and it was nice to see my dad cheering them on and being a positive male influence. He would bring me coffee to the games sit on the bleachers by me and smile. "Life's good, huh Sis?" he would say.

Something had to give. We couldn't keep going on like that. While I was deep inside my own pain trying to figure out what to do next with my life, Dad showed up at my door one day unannounced. This was strange because he always called before he came over. He begged me to go with him to pass out flyers for the business he ran with my mom. I couldn't figure out why this would be important so I refused, even as he kept after me, "Please Sis, go with me. I need to talk with you." I finally snapped at him and told him that I was busy, I was tired from getting up at 4:00 in the morning and I still needed to make dinner for my family.

I told him to take Shawn with him instead, so he hugged me and they left. When they returned it was late and Dad knew I was at my limit so he dropped Shawn at the front door and told him to always believe in himself no matter what happened. He told him, "Twenty years from now I want you to hug your Mom for me and tell her I love her." Shawn didn't tell me this until nineteen years later.

That night was the last time I talked to my father.

The next day at work, I was looking forward to a night at home with my kids. That changed the second I answered one phone call.

"Debbie, this is Pioneer Valley ER—it's your Dad, he's had a heart attack."

I felt a huge lump in my throat. I had to get to the hospital fast to see him.

8

DAD IS GONE
1986–1989

Grief knits two hearts in closer bonds than happiness ever can; and common sufferings are far stronger links than common joys.
—Alphonse de Lamartine

The call came while I was at work. I told my boss that my father had a heart attack, and then I left immediately. I wanted to hurry to the hospital, but first I needed to take care of my kids. I picked up Katy, who was almost two now, from daycare and the older children from school and brought them home. My brother-in-law came right away to take care of my babies, freeing me to focus completely on Dad.

Tears streamed down my face as I sped to the hospital. It's a wonder I didn't crash. When I finally reached the hospital, I ran charging through the doors in the ER; there in front of me was Mom, the look on her face told me I was too late—Dad had already passed away. At fifty-two, he had a massive heart attack and was gone within a half hour. My own heart shattered to fragments, and it would be years before I was able to piece them back together. He was too young to die and in the blink of an eye my rock, the one person I could lean on, was gone.

We had never exchanged many words. We didn't need to. Dad and I had a strong bond and an intuitive connection that transcended conversation. He always knew when I was feeling down and would somehow take on my burden, and I would feel a huge weight lifted off my shoulders.

We spent a lot of time together, just fishing or hanging out, especially after I told him what his brother had done to me. I think Dad was protecting me in his way. We never again discussed what my uncle had done to me, because Dad kept his promise to me that he would never bring it up again. He kept his word to the end and he died still keeping the promise he had made to me when I was just fifteen.

As a teen I was too busy rebelling to notice it, but by the time I was in my twenties, I had figured out that there was a silent connection between Dad and me. I could feel it. He would have a smile on his face, but I could see the hurt behind the smile. He had the ability to look right at me and feel exactly what I felt.

Whenever I couldn't cope any longer with my dysfunctional marriage, or with life in general, I would go to my dad's place, pour myself a cup of coffee, sit down with him at the kitchen table, and soak in his healing energy. All he had to do was take one look at me, and his eyes would immediately well up with tears. Intuitively, I could feel him saying to me, "It's OK, just let it go." Somehow, he took my burdens away and made me feel whole again. Then he would stand up and kiss me. "See you next time, Sis." That was it.

Mom always laughed and said, "You two just don't have many words to say to each other, do you?" Dad would chuckle at her comment. In silence, we had said it all.

Every Christmas, we had a family reunion with my father's family. In the summer, we also had a big summer picnic. As reluctant as I was to go, I always went for my father.

Of course, the uncle who raped me at age nine would be there.

Just knowing I'd have to see him made me sick to my stomach, and about an hour beforehand I always threw up. I couldn't eat when he was around. But I managed to cope.

I always brought my kids because I knew Dad enjoyed having them there. At times during these family celebrations, my father's face grew red with anger when my uncle came near him. I could sense an explosion about to happen, and it terrified me. I watched Dad closely, trying to tell him telepathically, *Don't, Dad, don't!* As if he heard, he glanced over at me, and that was it. He'd give me a wink, and his anger would disappear. It was paramount to Dad that he kept his promise to me. Silently, we helped each other through these episodes.

I survived these family gatherings because I knew my dad was right there by my side the entire time. He helped me carry the life burden of rape and the subsequent pain so I didn't have to do it alone. He watched over me, protecting my feelings and my heart.

With Dad gone, I didn't have that anymore. At his funeral I cried not only because I missed him, but also because I felt like a scared and lost little orphan, all alone. I could hardly stand to look at my uncle who was there. I hated him so badly. I didn't want him there at the funeral. I never wanted to see him again.

I stopped going to family reunions. I couldn't face my uncle without Dad nearby. I had never felt so alone in my entire life.

There's no rhyme or reason to grief. I was sad and hurt, but I was also angry with Dad for leaving me. It took me a long time to get over that anger. It took me even longer to get over the guilt I felt for being mad at him for leaving me alone, not waiting for me to say goodbye. I needed to tell him I was sorry for yelling at him the night before he died. I needed to tell him he was my hero and I loved him.

Two days after my dad's funeral I was at the Laundromat with

Katy and Wendy. I was leaning on a washer staring into space when I looked up to see an old man standing right in front of me. It startled me, but I looked right at him and saw something very familiar—he had my dad's eyes. Before I could say anything he smiled at me and said, "It's going to be ok, Sis!"

My heart sank as my eyes welled up with tears. I quickly looked around to see if anyone was looking and when I turned back, he was gone. I ran out the door and looked down the sidewalk. No one. I ran around the corner. No one. I ran back inside the Laundromat. No one. Wendy and Katy confirmed that the man had been there, but they never saw him leave.

This was my first encounter with my dad after he left this world. There would be many more. I'm not sure why he showed up as an old man, but I believe it was so he wouldn't frighten me. He never looked like that old man again—he looked just like himself.

Mom and Dad ran a storage unit together and when he died, she was fired almost immediately. The owners wanted two people to run the place, not my mother by herself. Dad had no insurance, which left Mom completely broke. I quit my job in order to collect the funds I had accumulated through profit sharing. I took that money and gave it to my mom because I desperately wanted to do something kind for her. Over the years I had shut her out of my life, but I still loved her. She was my mother and Dad's death had affected both of us deeply. I felt the need to reach out and connect with her through the pain we were both experiencing.

Unfortunately, that phase was short-lived, and my need to connect didn't last. Not long afterwards, I retreated once again. Mom was on the mend financially and she had found a new job and a new place to live. She seemed to be healing, at least that was the excuse I used, but I felt more broken than ever. I didn't know and didn't care at the time but mom was more broken than I could ever have been. The loss of my dad was more than she could bear to live with.

My relationship with my mom deteriorated quickly after that. It didn't help that after all of those years, my mother decided to finally confront my uncle, even though I had asked her not to. I was angry with her for going against my wishes. I had no desire whatsoever to relive that horrific experience and I wanted to keep that emotional wound closed forever.

I didn't realize it at the time, but she really was just trying to help me. She wanted to be part of my life and make right the wrong that was done to her daughter. She was also very lonely and heartbroken with the loss of my dad; she needed me. And maybe she was trying to put an end to generations of sexual abuse. At that time, I still didn't know she had been abused as a child. All I did know was that she had broken her promise. As a result, I shut her out more and more.

Now I was truly an emotional orphan, bereft of any support. I couldn't deal with losing my dad; the constant abuse my husband dished out; my growing sense of detachment from the world. I closed everybody out of my life, including my children.

In the end, I had a nervous breakdown. Emotionally I shut down, going numb. And I turned mean. History was repeating itself, and I watched myself following the pattern of my mother's behavior from my childhood. I turned mean not just to my mother and my husband, but also to my children—the most important people in my life. Whereas once I had nurtured and protected them, now I withheld my love from them. Deep-seated anger surfaced, resulting in me yelling uncontrollably at my kids. Pretty soon I was yelling and swearing and angry with everyone in my life. I was completely out of control. I needed an outlet and I found it in a co-worker. I totally fell in love with him, and we had a yearlong affair. I knew it was wrong, but I didn't care. At least I could feel again. Once again, shades of my mother's coping patterns.

When the affair finally ended, the feelings of worthlessness came rushing back. I had left my job to end the affair I was lost in. With no job and no one to love me, I spent the next two years barely existing, living in a fog, and numb to practically everything.

I began drinking—first wine and then hard liquor, suddenly

becoming an alcoholic. There was nothing left to live for. I had distanced myself from my children to the point where I couldn't pull myself out of my depressed state even for them. I had finally reached the point where I was ready to kill myself.

One day, the perfect opportunity presented itself. The kids were at school, Joe was at work and I was home alone. I went into our garage, closed the door, climbed into the driver's seat of my car and started the engine.

I'll be out of here in no time, I thought to myself.

Unfortunately, Joe came home early. He found me in the garage and immediately turned off the engine. I was so angry because he never came home early and it was bizarre to see him suddenly appear.

My husband began to weep. Somewhere inside of him was a human being. Through his tears, he asked me why I wanted to leave him. Even my suicide was about him. How myopic!

He had no clue that his behavior toward me was slowly killing me and that I was just trying to speed up the process.

Later that day, Dad's words came back to me. Time and again, he had seen how emotionally abused I was, and he made every effort to get through to me. I remembered how he would sit me down and ask, "How long are you gonna put up with this? When are you gonna stand up for yourself? You don't need to live this way. You're better than that." He always had words of encouragement for me.

One of his questions kept echoing through my mind: "When are you gonna see how truly beautiful you are?"

I didn't know when, or if, that day would ever come.

9

CAN IT GET WORSE?
1989–1990

During our lives we're faced with so many elements as well, we experience so many setbacks, and fight such a hand-to-hand battle with failure, head down in the rain, just trying to stay upright and have a little hope. The Tour isn't just a bike race, it tests you mentally, physically, and even morally. —Lance Armstrong

*M*aybe Dad's words were starting to sink in, because I finally picked myself up and found another job. I was hired at a large print house as a four-color stripper and plate burner. Going back to work gave me a positive and productive focus. At least it took me away from the depression and the alcohol I'd been abusing. Working made me feel human again. One thing didn't change, though: I was still mean and angry. I had developed a really bad attitude.

I loved my kids so much, but wasn't the mom they were used to. I didn't go to their school programs anymore and ignored them most of the time, even when they came to me for help with their problems. I was still so numb inside that I couldn't deal with anything. I was practically useless to my children. Barely four years old, little Katy suffered the most from my absence.

My energy level was so low that I became prone to catching colds and other bugs. I thought I had caught a particularly nasty flu because I was so weak, dizzy, and absolutely drained. After several weeks, the "flu" hadn't cleared up and I felt myself getting sicker and sicker. Finally, I made myself go to the doctor.

After I explained my symptoms, she proceeded to do a complete physical exam, including a PAP smear. I did not have a good feeling about this.

Later that week, the doctor called me. *Bad sign,* I thought. She explained that the results of my PAP smear had come back seriously abnormal and she wanted to see me right away. This was definitely more than the flu.

I tried to not give it much thought. In fact, I was more miffed about having to miss work again than I was concerned about my health, a sure sign of my depression. I made an appointment and prepared myself for whatever the doctor had to tell me.

I arrived at my appointment, and my doctor saw me immediately. She led me into her office and when she brought out my chart, I began to feel very uncomfortable.

"We need to do a biopsy," she said in a matter of fact tone.

I sat there confused. "What for?" I finally asked.

"You're showing signs of cancer cells on your PAP smear. We can't tell for sure unless we do a biopsy."

I couldn't believe this was happening. The conversation felt surreal. Cancer? I was only thirty-three years old. I didn't cry, just listened to the rest of what the doctor had to say with a sense of detachment. Part of me thought, *Okay, whatever. Maybe it's better this way. It is time for me to leave this world.*

Still, part of me wasn't ready for something as serious as cancer. My kids were too young. What would happen to them if I died? Despite my previous suicide attempt, I didn't feel ready to go. My intuition told me I needed to hang around and that things would be all right. My doctor scheduled a biopsy for the following week.

During the biopsy, I knew. Nobody had to tell me the results. I knew at that moment that I had cervical cancer without a doubt. I wondered what was next for me.

The doctor suggested that I go see a specialist who was from Denver. She was in Salt Lake City and she performed a laser surgery.

"It's a very new procedure", she explained, "but I want you to give it some thought, because it's either that or we go in cut it out. I don't know a whole lot about this laser surgery. I've been reading all I can find about it. If you're a willing victim, we'll go for it."

The doctor chose an interesting set of words when she gave me my options. The biopsy came back positive, as I expected. I decided I'd be a "willing victim" and try the newfangled laser procedure. *Why not?*

"I have cervical cancer," I told Joe that evening at home. He didn't believe me and I was shocked to hear him laugh.

"Yeah, right," he mocked. "You just have a *female* problem. They'll fix it." He treated me as if I was crazy.

"Did you hear what I just said to you?" I demanded.

"Don't screw with me," he threatened. "I gotta go to work tomorrow. You do your thing. Deal with your problem, whatever your problem is. Take care of it. I don't want to know."

I wasn't sure if he didn't care or if he was just too scared to deal with it. It was pointless to try to get through to him, though, so I dropped it. As usual, I was on my own.

My laser surgery was a month away. At first, I didn't give it much thought. But as the date loomed closer, I became frightened. Emotionally, I became a basket case. I needed somebody to talk to. Someone to commiserate with me, to say, "Oh my God, you have cancer!"

Joe wasn't that someone. He couldn't deal with it. Five days before I went into surgery, he packed his bags and disappeared. Right before he left, he said, "I'm leaving. I'm gonna go work somewhere. I'll call you."

I hated him for leaving me when I needed him the most. I was scared. I didn't want to do this. I didn't want to go by myself. I wanted somebody to hold me and say, "It's going to be okay."

Even though I had shut my mom out of my life since my dad

died, the reality was that she was all I had. One of the hardest things I ever did was pick up the phone and call my mom and tell her I had cervical cancer.

"I'm scared," I told her. "I don't want to go alone." And of course, she was right there.

Mom drove me to my surgery at the University of Utah in Salt Lake City. She waited patiently, keeping in touch with the neighbor who was watching the kids. She stayed there with me through the entire operation. The laser procedure was very new and I was one of the first women in the country to have it done.

It was a hellish experience from the start. The doctor performing the procedure had the worst bedside manner I'd ever seen. The surgery took forever, and it hurt unbearably, even with the cervical blocks I was given. I was awake throughout the entire procedure, lying there on the bed without whimpering or complaining.

After more than six hours of surgery, my legs went numb. I couldn't stand it anymore. My patience had run out. I looked at the surgeon and asked, "Are you just about done?"

She stood straight up and glared at me. "Why, you fu—ing crybaby!" she screamed. There I was, flat on my back, in tremendous pain, and my own doctor was swearing at me!

The assisting nurse, a woman in her early twenties, began to cry. Her tears kept flowing until she ran out of the room. The doctor started swearing at her, calling her a stupid bitch. She turned off the laser equipment; then she stomped to the operating room door, thrust it open, and yelled out, "Will somebody get in here?"

When the ordeal was over, my mother tried to catch the doctor in the hallway. "How is she, Doctor?" Mom asked. "How did the surgery go?" The doctor was indignant. She brushed my mom off and kept on walking. Mom didn't know where to turn.

Finally, Mom was taken to the room where I was recovering. She was relieved to see me doing okay. Another nurse, not the young one who had burst into tears, was taking care of me when the university hospital's head doctor came into my room with a couple of forms. He asked me if I would take a few moments to fill them out. Mom and I looked at the papers. They were complaint forms against my surgeon. Sure, I'd fill them out and with pleasure, I told the doctor.

While I recovered at the hospital, Mom stayed by my side. She took me home after I was discharged and, after getting me into bed, she went and picked up my children. She stayed with me several days, waiting on me since I couldn't move. She also took care of the kids—taking them to school, feeding and bathing them. I felt so ashamed. Why had I shut her out of my life?

Four days after my surgery, Joe came back, and Mom went home. Everything went back to the way it used to be. Joe acted as if nothing had happened. I acted as if my Mom wasn't a part of my life. Deep inside, I felt pathetic. How sad that after all she had done for me in my time of need, I couldn't bring myself to love my own mother.

Three years after my surgery, I was relieved that the cancer hadn't returned. But I still had problems. I experienced horrible, painful cramps that sent me home from work several times. I also frequently developed infections and had to be on antibiotics.

Finally, I went to a gynecologist to see what was wrong. I couldn't believe what he discovered: the laser surgery had damaged my uterus. The foul-mouthed doctor who had performed the procedure burned a hole through my cervix. The laser bumped my uterus and created a hole on the side of it, causing permanent damage. I was stunned. I had no idea any of this had happened.

My doctor asked me if I wanted to file a lawsuit. He offered to fill out an entire report for me. I didn't know what to do. I was close to leaving Joe. I was seriously ready to walk out on him. *Should I leave? Should I file a suit?*

In the end, I did nothing. I stayed with Joe, and I chose to not go through with the lawsuit against the doctor who had damaged me. Emotionally, I just wasn't capable of suing and I couldn't find the strength to fight.

My doctor told me that the damage was so extensive that I'd never be able to carry another baby. If I got pregnant, my body would abort the baby instantly. And if for some reason it didn't, the resulting infection would be so severe it would kill both of us. She urged me to have a hysterectomy.

Because I didn't have medical insurance, I told her I couldn't afford to have a hysterectomy. She explained that because of my financial hardship, we could make special arrangements with the hospital to have the hysterectomy done at a small fraction of the cost.

I declined even after she stressed the risks of constant pain and perpetual infection. The memory of my laser procedure was still vivid in my mind and I didn't want to go through another surgery. Instead, I went on birth control pills and hoped for the best.

The infections continued. Thankfully, antibiotics cleared them up quickly and I managed well enough for another six months. At 35, I became terribly sick, so sick that I thought the cancer had come back.

I went back to my doctor to find out what was going on and told her I thought the cancer had returned. She took one look at me and felt I could be right. I looked that bad.

She did a PAP smear and she also took a sample of my blood for more lab tests. At home, I was on pins and needles. I jumped every time the phone rang.

Two days later, my doctor called me. She gave me the results. I felt tears well up in my eyes. "Oh, my God!" I cried out loud.

I didn't have cancer. I was pregnant.

10

ANOTHER BLESSING
1990–1993

Courage is the art of being the only one who knows you're scared to death. —Earl Wilson

*M*y doctor had told me that if I got pregnant, my body would abort the baby instantly. Yet here I was, ten and a half weeks pregnant, against all odds. She also had said that if I didn't miscarry, I'd develop a horrendous infection that would kill both the baby and me. By all appearances, I was headed straight for that worst-case scenario.

My doctor felt there was only one solution: "We need to make an appointment for you at the abortion clinic," she said. "I know this is going to be horrible for you, but we have to do this. This child will kill you."

I didn't want an abortion. I preferred to just take my chances with the pregnancy.

My doctor was adamant, insisting that if I went ahead with the pregnancy neither my baby nor I would survive. She reminded me of my children at home; who would care for them if I died?

Her words hit my heart. Reluctantly, I agreed to go to the abortion clinic. When I returned home I told Joe what the doctor had told me, all he could say was "Good." *Good,* because he had never wanted any kids and we already had three. So two days later I was headed to the clinic on my own. My heart raced as I pulled into the clinic's parking lot. Fighting my instinct to run away, I breathed deeply as I opened the door and walked inside. Would my trembling stop?

I signed the papers and I sat through a frightening film that showed exactly what they were going to do to me on the operating table. I felt my stomach turning. I can't do this.

The movie ended, and a nurse escorted me into a room with a table and asked me to hop up and relax. I was alone. Only terror describes how one's insides turn to jelly lying there on the table. What was I doing? I didn't want to go through with the abortion.

I climbed down from the table and ran out of the clinic in tears.

Back in the car, I couldn't stop my tears. I sat there having a long conversation with God. "This is it," I said. "Take me with my child. I'd rather go with my baby than do this." After crying for a long time, I regained my composure and drove home.

Joe could not believe that I hadn't gone through with the abortion. "You went to the abortion clinic and chickened out. So now what?" he demanded.

"Well, I guess either I'm gonna have this baby, or neither one of us will make it," I replied.

"You're doing it on your own," he snapped back. "I didn't want any more kids. Good luck. Let me know how it goes."

My husband didn't talk to me for the next four months. In fact, he kicked me out of our bedroom. At least I had some peace and quiet on the couch in the living room.

During this time, I befriended a man at work. Ryce was in his early thirties and I was thirty-five; he quickly became a good friend to me. He was everything my husband wasn't. He was kind like a brother and he really listened as we talked together and hung out.

He was somebody with whom I could share the ups and downs of my pregnancy and enjoy fun, light moments.

Ryce took a genuine interest in me, wanting to know all about my life. He even wanted to rub my tummy and talk to the baby! He became such a good friend that he often came over to the house and had dinner with us. I thought Joe would care or wonder about him but he never did. He liked talking to him and was always glad when he showed up. It spared him from me trying to share with him. He knew we were friends and nothing more.

Little did I know that while I was falling in love with our friendship, Ryce was falling in love with me! He decided to confront my husband about his behavior toward me. On an evening when I wasn't home, Ryce came to our house and reprimanded Joe for mistreating me, then accused him of being a bad husband. Ryce confessed his love for me and revealed that he wanted to marry me and raise the child.

I didn't learn about this incident for two months after it took place. I felt hurt when I found out what he had done behind my back, even though he was right about Joe being a bad husband, he was supposed to be my friend. I knew why Joe never mentioned this—his ego would never admit another man questioned him. What I didn't know is that Ryce ever had those feelings toward me. Instead, I felt betrayed because I had shared everything with him. My feelings about being a mom, marriage, everything–how could he do this?

Joe simply told him, "Hey, whatever. If she loves you, she'll leave. But, you know she'll never leave me." He was so sure I'd stay with him through anything. Perhaps Joe was right. I had already stuck by him for fifteen years.

My fourth pregnancy was a difficult one. I was sick a lot, to the point of almost losing my job for missing too much work. I continued to sleep on the couch until I got so big that I couldn't sleep there comfortably anymore. I then moved to the dining room, where I slept on the floor with little Katy and occasionally Wendy. We curled up

Katy

together by the back door, which had a glass window and we watched the stars and the changing moon together until we all fell asleep.

At work they couldn't accommodate me anymore. I was eight months pregnant and so sick all the time that they made me quit my job temporarily to stay home in bed. The bad news was that I had no paychecks coming in even though they promised to hold the job for me until I was able to return. The good news was that I got the bed back. My doctor put me on bed rest and Joe let me have the bed; he slept on the couch.

Katy stayed by my side as much as she could. She was the Mom and I was the child. She waited on me and looked out for me most of the day. At night she slept with me. Shawn was sixteen and was in trouble a lot. At almost nine months pregnant, I had a hard time trying to keep track of him. He would stay out until dawn on some nights with me waiting up for him. He was arrested for breaking into cars a few times. Wendy was busy with her friends and never wanted much to do with me.

Shawn

When Shawn's best friend was killed in an accident, his life spiraled out of control. He started to get in trouble with the law repeatedly. Joe sent him to live with his uncle, Joe's brother, in Florida. He stayed for five months. It was awful not having Shawn home but I knew it was going to take something drastic to pull him through this. Wendy was getting more closed off to me the closer it came time for the baby. She did become closer to Katy though and I was very happy about it.

I went into labor at about 7:00 one night; we left Katy with Wendy and hurried to the hospital. I was very anxious and afraid, but I liked my doctor. She was gentle and compassionate. Best of all, she trusted my judgment and I trusted hers.

However, even she had doubts when, after ten hours of hard labor, nothing was happening. I wasn't dilating at all and she wanted to perform a C-section.

I begged her to wait. Having had my first three kids through natural childbirth, I planned to do the same with my fourth. Each time my doctor mentioned Cesarean, I told her, "No, I need to wait."

She was flustered and confused. "Why won't you listen to me?" she asked.

"Because I know God will make it okay." I was certain of it. She thought I was wacko, but thankfully, she believed me anyway.

"Debbie . . . "

"Please, just listen to me. It'll be okay."

The doctor finally shook her head and walked out of the room. *Good, I just bought myself more time,* I thought.

After eleven hours of labor, she checked me again. "I'm sorry, Debbie," she said firmly with a look of concern on her face. "I have to override your decision."

I was absolutely exhausted, but I wasn't ready to give up. I took a long look at my doctor. Then I said out loud, "Okay, God, now. I can't do this anymore. It needs to happen right now." Reluctantly, my doctor checked me again. She couldn't believe what she saw. I was completely dilated, and the baby was crowning! I let out a quiet "thank you" and started to cry.

I had been thinking a lot about my dad, first throughout my pregnancy and now during labor. He had held my three older ones, but he would never hold little Nancy. From the start I knew this baby was a girl. I wanted to name her Glen after Dad, but I figured she wouldn't be happy to have a boy's name. I named her after my late mother-in-law instead.

Dad's spirit came to see me all the time, but since he was no longer of this earth he wouldn't be able to hold my daughter, and this troubled me greatly. I said to Dad, "Okay, I know that you come and see me. I know this. I know in my heart that you're here all the time, but I need a physical sign that you know this baby, that you *know* her. That you held her." It was important to me that my baby and my Dad have a bond.

When Nancy was born, my doctor wiped her off and held her up for me to see. "Oh my God," she said, "Look at that red hair!" I smiled. Nancy had the same flaming red hair my father once had. That was the sign I'd been looking for. The funny thing was that Nancy's red hair didn't last. Within three months, her hair turned brown, and it's been brown ever since. But at the moment of birth it was bright red, letting me know that my Dad was a part of Nancy's life just like he continued to be a big part of mine.

Nancy was absolutely delightful. I spent hours on end holding her. Wendy and Katy were tickled pink to have a baby in the house—at least for a little while. The excitement didn't last long. Wendy still hated me and tried hard not to love her baby sister. She stayed close to Katy during this time and was always looking after her. My friend Ryce filled in for Joe, who didn't want to be there. He came over frequently and spent time with me, Nancy, Katy and Wendy. Although I kept our friendship at a distance, I was thankful for his caring company.

I found a good sitter and went back to work. I was glad to be able to work again without getting sick all the time. Shawn was gone much too long and my heart ached from worrying about him. I wanted him home and I wanted him to meet his baby sister. Wendy would play with the baby when she thought I wasn't looking. I would watch as she sang to her and held her close. Ryce was still very present and he loved to hear my stories about the baby. Every day I couldn't wait to tell him what she was doing next.

During these times, it was often so bad at home I would find myself loading the girls into the car in the middle of the night on the weekends and running away. Inevitably I would end up on Mom's doorstep. She followed in Dad's footsteps, careful not to question why I was there. I would curl up on her couch with Nancy while Mom would tuck Wendy and Katy in her bed. On one of those nights I listened as Mom was tucking the girls in. Wendy asked her grandma why her daddy didn't love us. I listened as my mother answered, trying to keep her voice steady. I knew she was fighting back her own tears. Mom told Wendy that her daddy loved her the best way he knew how. She kissed them good night and told them both how much they meant to her and how much she loved them.

The months passed, and the holidays rolled around. It was time for our annual Christmas party at work. Joe and I left the girls with a sitter and went to the party. Ryce went, too. We all had way too much to drink, and before I knew it, Joe's sexual addiction kicked in again. He was talking to Ryce and me about us having a three-some and Ryce actually said he'd be willing to try it.

I was sickened and crushed. Right then and there, I ended my friendship with Ryce and stormed out of the party, got in my car, and drove off. I stopped in the middle of nowhere and desperately looked around. I found a rag in the car, grabbed it, walked outside, and shoved it into the car's tailpipe. I sat back inside the car with the engine running and waited. I felt myself lose control. My bladder let go and I peed all over myself. My body let go, and I felt my spirit drift away. I thought for sure this was it. I was dead.

Through the haze, my father's voice came through loud and clear. "You need to stop this now," he said with authority. Thankfully, I listened.

Somehow I managed to open the car door and stumble out onto the snow. I lay there crying on the cold ground, my hot tears melting the snow. After the dizziness passed, I got up and turned off the car engine. I walked to the back of the car and pulled the rag out of the tailpipe, got back into the driver's seat and drove myself home.

The next week, I found a counselor.

Shawn came home a week later. He finally met his baby sister; he cried as he held her. Time went by and I stayed numb. I didn't have any friends and life was easier that way. I stayed busy with work and absorbed with advancing my career. Shawn was working at the mall and liking it. One night he called me from work and pleaded with me to come down to the mall. He had seen a girl that he was dying for me to check out. I packed up Nancy, left Katy with Wendy and took off to the mall. I hid behind a rack of clothes at my son's request as he pointed out the girl who worked across the hall. Shawn thought that she was beautiful and I urged him to ask her to dinner. Six months later he finally mustered up enough nerve to ask her out and they dated regularly after that. I knew he loved her and so did I.

While Shawn was happy and dating Sarah, Wendy was struggling. She had shut me out of her life, refusing to share anything with me. She blossomed into a beautiful young woman, afraid of herself and still hating me. However, she was still close to Katy and now Nancy, which gave her some comfort at home. There was a boy in school she had a crush on over the summer vacation and when school started back up it got more intense. At Halloween he asked her to the Christmas dance. I watched as she told me, and her face glowed—so did mine because she was finally sharing with me. As Thanksgiving drew near, Wendy asked me if she could go and spend the weekend in Michigan with her best friend who had moved there a year ago. She said her parents were buying her a ticket to fly and she wanted to go so badly. With some reservations about allowing her to fly alone, I finally agreed.

Wendy

While she was in Michigan, the boy she had such a crush on, the young man who had asked her to the Christmas Dance, was killed in a car accident along with three of her other friends. The accident was the day after Thanksgiving and I knew I couldn't get her on a flight home in time for the funeral. I chose to tell her when she returned home, so I could be with her when I broke the news. She hated me for it, and she still does. She shut me out completely after that.

Joe and I sold our house in Kearns and moved into a nicer home in West Jordan. I thought maybe this time my life was going to turn around finally. Our new home was beautiful. With an acre of land, it was everything I had always wanted. Our new start and Dad's presence gave me the strength to stand up to Joe and his sexual addiction.

"Don't you ever bring anyone home again!" I said to him. "That's it. You're done. I'm never doing this again."

God that felt good! I was finally reclaiming a part of my soul.

I even found the courage to ask Joe to leave. He wouldn't hear it, though. "You're stuck with me forever," he replied. "I will never leave you. If you want out of this marriage, it's you that's gonna walk out, not me. You're gonna look like the bad guy. I will never do that." That was the first time we ever talked seriously about getting a divorce.

Ryce wanted our friendship back. He wrote me a long, soulful letter asking for forgiveness and for a second chance. But I felt I couldn't trust him anymore. In truth, I didn't trust anybody. I told Ryce I never wanted to talk to him again. Our friendship was broken, and nothing could fix it. I quit my job and got a new one working for a different company. This was a hard decision for me to make, but I knew it was the right one. Someday I was going to make it. I wanted to be somebody. I wanted to be rich and to do that I needed to be on my own, independent. I buried myself in work again. Shawn, at 23, was married to Sarah and on his way to Hawaii with his bride. Wendy, at 19, was engaged to her boyfriend, Jeremy. Katy was a happy kid with a lot of friends. She did well in school and kept a close eye out for Nancy. Nancy was just Nancy—she played with her sister Katy a lot. It seemed that my children were happier than they had ever been.

Despite all the changes I made in my life, I still felt awful. I was sinking back into a dark hole and I didn't know how to climb out. I didn't like who I was at all and thought I had turned into a demon. I felt like one. I felt evil. I could feel my soul changing, turning black as though it was rotting. I was dying from the inside out. Everything felt so dark and bleak. I'd given into fear and reached the point of hopelessness.

Others could see the change in me, too. A work friend, Gerry, became concerned. "What's wrong with you?" he asked. "The light in your eyes is disappearing." That hurt, but I knew he was right. He could see it in my eyes, and I could feel it in my soul.

Gerry tried to reach me. Every so often he'd remind me, "Your light's turning off. What are you gonna do?" He tried, but he couldn't help me. My light was going out. I could feel it. I hated who I had become.

One night on my way home from work, I stopped at the store. I'd had enough. *I'm leaving this place,* I told myself. *I'm not doing my children any good. I don't even notice them anymore. I can't feel that they love me. I don't feel anything. I'm dead.*

I went in and took a bottle of sleeping pills off the shelf. Not enough in here, I thought. So I bought two bottles. I read the instructions carefully, and then drove home. Nobody else was around and the house was still and empty. I grabbed a bottle of vodka from my kitchen, went into my bedroom, locked the door, poured myself a drink and sat on the bed. I opened the first bottle of pills and swallowed them in one gulp. They tasted so bad I almost threw up. I washed them down with vodka and sat there for ten minutes before I started to panic. *Oh my God, what have I done?*

I forced those feelings away, telling myself to just shut up and finish it. Negative thoughts filled my mind. *I don't want to be in this body anymore. I don't want to be here. I can't stand who I am.* Everything I had done . . . every horrible thing I had done . . . abandoning my children . . . the affair . . . all the awful things I let Joe do . . . I just couldn't bear it anymore.

I knew that what I was doing was wrong, that after leaving this world I'd have to explain myself, and why I chose to do what I did. I just could not stand my pain any longer. I couldn't. I opened the other bottle and took the rest of the pills.

I lay down and cried. I wondered where my children were. Shawn, I knew, was happily married and doing well. Wendy was engaged, but I didn't know how she would fare. Katy was eight and Nancy was three, they were still babies but they'd probably be all right in the long run. Katy was at school; Nancy was in daycare.

I blacked out, but not completely. I felt reality slipping away. It felt good to have everything go completely numb. I felt released from all the emotional pain I'd been carrying for so long. But it didn't last. Hard as I tried, I couldn't stay in that state of numbness. All the ugliness and hurt I was trying to escape came back to me with a vengeance. I felt everything turn dark and I was scared.

I closed my eyes and immediately felt better. The darkness started to fade away. In its place, a light appeared and began to grow. I wasn't afraid anymore. The light grew until it was huge and beautiful. I felt excited and I knew at that moment that God didn't hate me. He loved me.

I opened my eyes, expecting to be out of this world. To my surprise, I saw doctors and nurses standing around me—but the light remained. I realized what had happened. I had passed out from the pills, and somebody brought me to the hospital where my stomach was pumped. *How long had I been out of it?*

There was an oxygen mask over my face to help me breathe, while the medical team was busy monitoring my vital signs. Through it all, the beautiful light remained. I could see it glowing in the room. I looked at one of the doctors and told him I was going to be okay. He asked me, "Do you know what you did?"

I replied, "Yes. I brought God back with me." He didn't say a word, but one of the nurses smiled at me. She understood.

The doctor made me see the resident counselor the next morning. She and I had a good talk. The counselor told me not to lose that light. "I don't want to see your face in here again," she said. "You get to go home now, and you get to explain things to that little girl who came in here with you."

I gasped. "What little girl?" I asked. I was praying that it was Nancy, who would be too young to remember any of this. But it wasn't. "That beautiful little blond with the curls who's so broken," said the counselor. She was talking about my little Katy.

"You made a bad mistake," she continued. "You need to fix it. Now go home." Joe came to get me at the hospital, leaving Katy at home all by herself. When I walked through the doorway, she didn't run up to me; she didn't hug me. My little caregiver was deeply hurt and angry.

Facing her was painful. I sat down next to her and for the first time in years, took a good look at her. I felt her fear and her anger. She looked straight into my eyes and asked, "Where did you think you were going?"

I told her I wasn't going anywhere. She said, "You hurt me, Mommy. I was scared." I wrapped my arms around her and told her I wouldn't leave her again. I told her I was sorry. But, I felt her body stiffen up. She was not going to forgive me, not at that moment, anyway.

It's hard to look at what you've done and be accountable for the actions you take. Sometimes they hurt you forever and sometimes there's no forgiveness. As I held my little Katy, I knew that ours was not a normal mother-daughter relationship. We seemed to be connected by pain. But because it was our bond, it was sacred, and I embraced it. As Katy grew, so did her world of pain. When she's ready to release the pain and give it back to me, I'll be ready and willing to take it away from her.

11

STEPPING UP AND OUT
1993–1995

Don't be afraid to take one large step because you can't cross a chasm in two small leaps.—David Lloyd George, British Prime Minister and Statesman

*K*aty was the one who had found me after I passed out from swallowing two bottles of sleeping pills washed down with vodka. She came home from school with little Nancy, put her in front of the TV to watch cartoons, and then came to my room to check on me. When she found my bedroom door locked, Katy went around through the back yard to the sliding glass door that opened to my room. The door was unlocked and she entered quietly.

"Mom!" she called repeatedly. I was unresponsive. Frightened, eight-year-old Katy got on the phone and dialed her father's cell phone. "Mom won't wake up!" Joe was just pulling in the driveway; he hurried in and hauled me to the hospital.

My Katy was the one who saved my life. I was ashamed of what I had done. How could I have allowed this to happen? My little girl, whom I was supposed to take care of and protect, was the one who rescued me from my suicide attempt. Having to face my child and account for what I had done was the most humiliating moment of my life. I didn't see how I could sink any lower and I felt I had completely failed her.

Things were quiet on the home front for a while after that. Joe didn't have much to say. Shawn was still in Hawaii on his honeymoon and Wendy was working and still not speaking to me. Katy and Nancy didn't say much, either. It's as if they were all silently keeping an eye on me, making sure I wasn't going to try to do it again.

When Shawn and Sarah came back from their honeymoon, they came and went, much like I had done with my parents when I was a teen mom and wife. He was a quiet, sensitive young man. The older he got, the more he reminded me of my dad. .

But Shawn's childhood was catching up with him. Even when a parent is abusive, the child longs for a relationship with him. Such has been the case with Shawn. He moved out, but he remained under Joe's strong influence. My son worked for his dad, and in all his interactions with Joe I could see Shawn striving to do everything the way his father expected him to do it. But Joe constantly called Shawn a loser and told him he couldn't do anything right, yet our son still hung in there trying to be the perfect image of what his father expected.

Joe was never cruel with Wendy. Instead, he was protective of her. She got away with all kinds of stuff: throwing huge parties, piercing her nose, and doing other crazy teen things. Aside from her rebellious outbursts, though, she also tried hard to live up to Joe's expectations. Just like Shawn, Wendy was very much controlled by her father. She also strived to be the perfect image of what her dad expected, and she did everything she could to win his love.

Joe was the hardest on Katy. He was not protective of her as he was with Wendy. Katy was treated more like her brother; the only difference was that her beatings were less severe. Joe never punched her as he had Shawn. But he threw her against the wall a few times and spanked her too hard.

In reality you could count on the fingers of one hand the times the kids took severe physical abuse, but the smacking around, verbal abuse and the fear were always present! Katy was afraid of her dad, but she refused to show it. She was defiant and held her emotions inside, hidden from everyone's view. Often she would stand right up to her father and say, "Go ahead, beat me. I don't care." If he hit her or yelled at her, she'd just turn and walk away without crying. She just kept her hurt and rage bottled up deep inside.

For the most part, Joe ignored Nancy. He neglected her completely when she was a baby and continued to do so until she was a little older and demanded his attention. But she and I had a special bond. Together we had made it through an improbable pregnancy that was supposed to kill us both, and that connected us in a powerful way. I brought her with me everywhere I could, even to work. Between us, it was laughter and giggles and pure joy.

When Nancy started kindergarten, I was free to grow again professionally. I loved my work because I could excel there. I worked for a printing company; in addition to running the printing press, I was responsible for a large share of the office work. The responsibility made me feel important. I was messing up at home, but at work, I was doing it right! Joe hated my strength at work because it was a threat to him and his control over me. He knew it was slipping away.

Soon I became the office co-manager of this shop, and my responsibilities continued to grow. After I had worked there three years, my boss convinced me that I needed to be doing something better. He believed in me, and told me that I was capable of doing much more. He wanted to see me make more money and do something I really enjoyed, so he urged me to go into sales.

I was ready for the challenge. I transferred to the corporate office, which was at a downtown location, and started my career selling printing equipment, supplies, and services to healthcare facilities. I loved it. I worked with doctors and nurses, and it was great fun.

For a while, the chaos at home subsided. My kids had reached a place of greater stability. Life seemed to smooth out a bit for us.

This is not to say that everything was suddenly perfect. Joe and

I continued to fight because we never saw eye to eye on anything. He still worked hard to control me and I was like a robot around him. I kept my opinions to myself because sharing them meant being called stupid and suffering a three-hour-long lecture. My way of defying him was to excel as much as I could at work. The more I climbed the corporate ladder, the madder he became.

The company I worked for outsourced its smaller, more specialized printing jobs to a small printer who could fill this niche. That's how I met my friend Gary. He owned the small printing press with which we did business, and I was the person who worked directly with him. The first time I walked into his shop, he was at his desk. He stood to shake my hand and when he grabbed it I had the strangest feeling. Before he could say anything, I asked if we had met before. He smiled as he said no and I felt a sense of *deja vu* in the strangest way. It took me a minute to regroup and introduce myself, and by then he was chuckling under his breath thinking *Oh boy another dipstick.* This was the start of a beautiful friendship.

At first we didn't get along at all. We argued a lot, but over time a nice workplace friendship developed—aside from him teasing me about being an airhead. To say he encouraged me would be an understatement. He pushed as hard as he could for me to get out there and build my sales base to generate more business. I liked him because he believed in me and in my potential. He talked to me about the way to approach clients. He always answered my questions without judgment. To Gary, there was no such thing as a stupid question. He told me that I was brilliant and encouraged me every step of the way. With Gary cheering me on, I had the courage to branch off and go into business for myself. I became a printing services broker.

My new job was with a joined broker business with 600 other brokers. This career move infuriated Joe and he let me know it in no uncertain terms. He told me that I had just destroyed every effort on his part to make sure our family had food on the table. He told me over and over what a fool I was being and that I had no idea how to run my own business. He told me I was way too stupid to succeed.

I didn't care what he said. I knew that I would make it! Something inside me shook with eagerness, and it was an unrest that I could not control. I was hell bent not only on proving him wrong, but I was also going to be someone my dad would be proud of-someone I would be proud of.

I no longer had a steady paycheck, which scared me to death. Yet, working on commission made it possible for me to earn more money than I'd ever made before.

I went all out. I made phone calls, told prospective clients what I could provide, explained my background and experience, and shared who some of my clients were. Little by little, both my supplier base and my client base grew.

I was proud of myself for taking this big leap. Somehow I just knew that this was what I wanted to do. I was scared, but I was determined to make it work. The first two years were difficult. I ran into some unexpected obstacles, like losing a portion of my clientele due to non-compete contracts I had with my previous employer. But I kept moving forward with the business.

Gary watched me struggle. He knew that the first two years would be a testing period and a time when I would either roll up my sleeves and give it everything I had, or else give up and quit. I was never much for quitting, I wanted to make it work, I knew I had to. I just kept going, kept selling, and kept knocking on doors trying to build my business into a success. Gary encouraged me, serving as my source of strength whenever I got discouraged.

I finally got my big break when an amusement park signed on with me. After our initial eight-month contract was up, they signed a new, two-year contract with me, insuring a steady stream of income. Soon I was able to attract and sign contracts with more big companies.

Sometimes when business wasn't going too well, I'd stop by Gary's shop, sit down with a cup of coffee and share my woes with him. He was a terrific listener. After I unloaded, he would give me a pep talk. "You can do this," he always said. "What are you waiting for? Get out there and take care of it. You're experienced and knowledgeable."

When he encouraged me, my outlook improved tenfold. The whole scene reminded me of sitting with my father at his kitchen table many years ago. It felt great having a mentor again.

Gary's encouragement was the complete opposite of what I encountered at home. I had built my business to the point where I was making $40,000 a year, and all my paychecks went straight to our household expenses.

Joe told me I wasn't doing my part, never did anything to help and that I never made any money. I became so discouraged, believing I didn't contribute to our family at all. *Why did I listen to this? Why did I believe him? What mysterious glamour did his abuse hold for me?*

I wanted so badly for him to recognize me, and my accomplishments. Instead, I received the dreaded lecture about getting off my ass and getting a real job. Joe's words were a broken record that I couldn't turn off. He would replay these tapes and create the same drama, repeatedly, day in and day out. His prison was my prison. One of us had to break out.

At work, my confidence soared. I had been working on my own for four years and making it. I was doing very well for myself. Corporate meetings were twice a year and I was actually getting recognition for the progress I had made. These meetings were with 600 other brokers out on own and they took place in Minnesota. So not only was I out working for myself, I was also traveling twice a year. This just added to the fire at home. But I started to love my independence, believing in myself like I had never experienced before in my life.

At home, my confidence kept getting zapped. Joe hated the meetings and didn't want me to attend them. He hated that I was gone for a week at a time and that he had to take care of the kids. He called me non-stop, checking up on me, suspicious that I was partying. At one point, the hotel manager lost his patience because Joe constantly yelled at him for not sending somebody out to find me. Joe couldn't stand not knowing exactly where I was.

Wendy became the responsible homemaker. She took care of her little sisters and cooked; she also cleaned and tried to stay in school.

I desperately needed a friend; Gerry and Gary were both there for me. Gerry was alone as I was and we would meet up at the meetings in Minnesota to share news. Neither of them would let me feel sorry for myself. "Why are you sitting around whining?" one of them would ask. "Look at what you've built up. You're doing it!" Without both of their support, I never would have succeeded.

While I was busy finally making a life for myself, Joe's life went downhill fast. I was slipping away and he could feel that he was losing his control over me and didn't like it one bit. His sexual addiction was still going strong, but I had reached a place of strength where I could simply say no to his bizarre fantasies and walk away.

The result was that he became more vindictive. When he came home from work, he would snap at me. When we sat on the back patio with a cup of coffee, he'd lecture me endlessly.

He was determined to make me feel like a failure. Part of me felt like I was doing great. Part of me did, indeed, feel like I was failing. *Why did I keep listening to it?* Perhaps that question gnawed at my gut more than hearing Joe go on endlessly.

Joe tried to kill himself several times. He drank heavily every night. He would hide in the garage for hours, withdrawing more and more into himself. The garage became some sort of strange personal refuge for him. As his absence from my life increased, his violence towards me decreased. He couldn't accept his wife being successful in the world of business. He didn't know how to handle my growing success and confidence.

Professionally I was on top of my game, but personally I still wasn't living an exemplary life. I had several one-night stands that meant nothing to me. I felt nothing about having sex with these men. Emotionally, I was like the "walking dead."

Other than my children, the only person I felt anything for was Gary. We had a pure friendship. He gave me strength to grow my business. In exchange I tried to be there for him through his personal problems, first an ugly divorce and then conflicts with a string of girlfriends. Secretly, I was jealous of his girlfriends. Against my will and intention, I found myself falling in love with Gary.

I started to despise myself again. I thought of myself as a whore because I slept with men I picked up at bars. I saw myself as a bad mother because, even though I hated Joe's behavior, I became more like him every day, yelling at my kids and abusing them verbally. I started drinking more heavily. I didn't want to do any of this.

What was happening to me? Why couldn't I stop myself?

I had so many questions, no answers, feelings of despair and success, and hung on anyway.

Through it all, the only thing that made me feel alive was being in love with Gary. One day I came home from work, slumped down on the kitchen floor, and poured my guts out to Joe. "I haven't loved you in a long time," I told him. "I'm in love with Gary."

Joe replied, "I don't care, as long as you don't sleep with him. I don't care what you do. You can be in love with whoever you want, just don't go anywhere."

I cried uncontrollably because it hurt so badly to be married to one person while being in love with somebody else. I was so confused. I totally lost sight of who I was. I looked at myself in the mirror and hated what I saw.

Gary had been dating somebody on and off. When she finally moved in with him, reality hit. I was in love with a man, my best friend, who lived with another woman. I was married to a man whom I no longer loved, and who didn't love me, but who would never let me go. Nothing made sense. I needed to try something new, because so far nothing was working.

During one of the conventions I attended, Gerry listened intently as I told him that the walls were caving in. He asked me if I remembered the training he had mentioned four years earlier.

He had told me about an intense training session in Idaho, sort of a boot camp for people who need a wake up call, that went far beyond your average training. They called it life training.

What did I have to lose? He asked me to think about it since my light was almost completely gone. One month after the convention I found myself contemplating another suicide. I picked up the phone and called Gerry. I started to cry when he answered. He said, "Hi cutie, are you ready to rock and roll?"

"I'm ready. Sign me up."

1 2

S P E C T R U M
1995

Since we cannot change reality, let us change the eyes which see reality.—Nikos Kazantzakis

Two weeks after calling Gerry to ask for help, I started the first level of "Spectrum" training. In my entire life I'd never done anything quite like this. Sure, I'd gone to counselors, but this training was entirely different, even frightening. It was supposed to be. I explained the training to Joe and the kids and they all listened and asked many questions. Joe protested and said there was no way he would pay for it. At this point I didn't care what he said and I had already paid for it with my credit card. I looked at him with a calmness that he understood and told him I was going. I packed my bag, gave Wendy instructions for the girls, and got on a plane to Boise, Idaho.

The first phase was a four-day weekend session, with each day starting at nine and going for seventeen hours until two in the morning! Four days straight of intense training and sleep deprivation was grueling emotionally, mentally and physically. Using a variety of techniques including hypnotherapy and meditation, this first level took each participant back through their past. All of those painful memories I had long suppressed began to surface. I relived in full and vivid color the horrifying realities of my uncle raping me.

At the end of each day I was wiped out. I'd return to my hotel room, collapse onto my bed, and cry. I sobbed so hard I could barely breathe. I honestly did not know if I would survive this training, because the emotional pain it brought forth was excruciating.

Reliving those awful experiences from long ago suddenly made me a vulnerable nine-year-old child again, which frightened me. The only reason I kept going was that I knew I'd come out of this experience a stronger, and hopefully, a better, person.

The first day began with thirty trainees gathered in a large room for a group session. One by one, we shared our stories and the reasons we were here. I was ready to tell everybody what a horrid, wretched person I had become, so many words poured out.

By the time I was through, I was convinced the others thought I was one of the worst people on earth. It didn't matter that I was convinced of that myself and I needed to bare my soul.

By the end of the first day about a third of the participants were eliminated. Either they walked out on their own or they were asked to leave because of their drug or alcohol addictions. These people were urged to get help elsewhere; about twenty-two people remained. I was relieved my drinking problem did not control me to the extent that I could not go without a drink during the training. I wasn't thrilled with the rules, but I understood them.

That first night in the hotel room was the first time in years I wrote in my journal:

Dear God,
Well, here I am, I'm scared I don't know why I am here or what the hell I'm doing. I hate Joe—it's his fault, I hate his guts, I hate him I hate him I hate him I hate him! I hate Me I hate Me IHATE MEMEME!!!! I hate me I hate Me ME ME ME ME
Help Me God. Where are you? Do you still listen?

Step by step, the staff walked us through our memories. Every day, we did what they called a "stretch," which triggered an opening deep in my soul. The first stretch I encountered was standing in the middle of a circle with everyone else around me. Then I had to sing at the top of my lungs a song that was assigned to me by the facilitators. This was difficult for me. I have a horrible voice and I don't like to be embarrassed. But I did it!

Afterward I cried. To do something so embarrassing and not to care what other people were thinking was very freeing. Little did I know, what was ahead.

During one particular stretch, I had to close my eyes and imagine myself as a child. Along the way I became that child, and every scary event of my childhood came boiling out of me when I least expected it. I was terrified and felt out of control. I hid in a corner screaming.

When I was hiding, I felt someone's hand grab mine and pull me to my feet. He held me and told me to tell him what I was seeing. He kept telling me it was ok, just let it all out and he was present. I cried hysterically in his arms until there were no more tears left.

When it was over I remembered everything as if it had happened yesterday—all the fear and the anger of losing Dad, how cold his body was, like an ice cube . . . no, colder than that. He looked as if he were sleeping except he was purple. I shook him over and over, "Dad!" I cried, "Wake up!" I knew he was gone but the shock was more than I could bear.

All of these feelings came back just as intensely as the day it happened. I was so afraid and so pissed off all at the same time. I had exploded and was still in one piece, even more whole. Amazing!

During another portion of the training, I envisioned myself holding Dad in my arms and telling him everything I didn't get to say to him before he died. I hadn't realized I was holding so much anger inside. I was still mad at my father for leaving me, and all of that came pouring out during this session. Pretty soon, the story of my uncle raping me also came out.

At that point, I was taken out of the group setting and led

into a private session with two caring facilitators. They walked me through the whole ordeal with my uncle, helping me get through the anger so that I could grieve and ultimately find a place of healing. I walked out of that session with total recall of each detail of my uncle's vile act.

I was surprised by how many memories I had suppressed over the years; at the same time, I was not surprised at all.

For the first time in my life, all of the scattered pieces were falling into place; the mosaic was becoming whole. I saw how my uncle's actions had affected me, influencing the choices I made early in my life. I also saw how everything that I hated about my mother was also present in me: I had become my mother. This meant I also hated everything about me. That was my biggest "Aha!" moment of the entire weekend. Without realizing it, the traits and behaviors I found unacceptable in my mother had made their home in my life!

At the end of the four days I returned home knowing that I had to come to terms with this big issue. There was a two-week break before the second level of training was to begin.

This was a tough period, since home was no sanctuary for me. I was dealing with not only new realizations about myself, but also a husband who didn't understand what I was experiencing in personal growth. Joe was afraid of the changes he was seeing in me, More specifically, Joe was afraid of me. He didn't know how to respond when I stood up to his rude remarks and his name-calling. I told him that I wouldn't tolerate his mouth. If he couldn't stop himself, he needed to leave—which he did a lot in the next two weeks. The kids were shocked by my honesty. I told Shawn that I wanted him to start treating Sarah with more respect because he was acting like his father. I had long talks with Wendy about getting married. Wendy was upset about several things. She didn't like being responsible for her sisters and made it clear she wanted me to work things out with her dad. She did talk with me when I asked her to. We started to make plans together for her August wedding. Katy was very scared and not very responsive to me, but she was there. She was still mad because her security had been interrupted. As awful as home life could be, the kids were used to it and understood it. Nancy was the only one of our children who enjoyed her time with me.

I cried a lot during those two weeks away from the seminar, sometimes hysterically. In the first level of the spectrum training, the facilitators helped me knock down a few of the walls of anger, hate, and numbness I'd carefully built around me for protection. With these walls gone, I started to find my real self again.

For many years, I'd forgotten what it was like to actually love my children. Now I was remembering the joy I found in them. A gentler, softer side of me emerged. I stopped yelling at my kids, and hugged them much more often. They gave me weird looks, but I could tell they liked my behavioral changes. I also sensed their fear that these changes for the better might not last. I was told not to share the training process with anyone, so explaining it to my kids was a challenge. They waited patiently during these two weeks, wondering what was happening to me. I was very glad Shawn was married because Sarah occupied his time. They were expecting their first child. He had his own life to deal with and seemed accepting of what I was doing. Shawn, in a lot of ways, was the hardest of my children to deal with. He didn't like change, but he was an adult and needed to accept that he couldn't control my life, or his own, for that matter. Life just happens, control just cripples you from dealing with it.

I felt real love toward Joe for the first time in a long time, much as I'd felt when we first fell in love. All the love I once had for him, rushed back to me. I wanted to hold him and be held.

Unfortunately, unlike the kids who usually hugged me back, Joe was not able to return my love. He could not hold me. He would not hug me. I was happy to remember the love I'd felt for my husband. On the other hand, being "home" didn't feel right anymore. This mix of feelings seemed strange, yet I was stronger and could finally explore this trail of freedom that was emerging.

I poured my heart into my work in the two weeks between

training. I visited my clients with a new enthusiasm. I was ready to rock! I stopped by Gary's shop and explained to him what I was doing and he listened intently. When I was done, he hugged me, told me that he knew it would be ok, and that he was happy that I was finally learning to believe in myself. He said he would take care of the work I had in the shop and not to worry.

My marriage was not as easy. Joe demanded that I drop out of the training, but I refused. For the first time in our marriage, I was standing up to him. I learned in these two weeks that he had never loved me. It was like a light suddenly turning on. He couldn't love me. He didn't know how to love. I suddenly felt such a huge sorrow. I had spent twenty-four years of my life with a man who had never loved me, and he would never love me. It was time for me to live, and it was time to find out who I was. When the two weeks were up, I couldn't wait to go back to Boise. I told Joe he was going to be responsible for his kids for the first time in his life. I made it known that the responsibility wasn't going to fall on Wendy this time. He would have to do it himself. I told him if he couldn't handle it, I was leaving and would never come back. I was done living the way we had for way too long. I think the shock of me being so defiant was enough for him not to argue. I packed my bag for the second trip, told Katy it would be ok, kissed Nancy, and had a long talk with Wendy. She was relieved to hear the burden of her sisters was no longer hers. Katy was still scared and Shawn was glad that his new baby would actually have a grandma that could love her. Although he was still uncertain, he accepted it for now. Nancy simply didn't understand why everyone was upset. I told my children goodbye and was on my way back to Boise.

I went to "level two" training, ready for whatever might come. I bubbled over with anticipation for the growth and changes that surely would happen at this next stage. The training became my safe haven where I could explore and release feelings trapped inside me. Only there, it was acceptable to be the real me, with nobody criticizing me for what I felt or what I said.

During the second level, I went through a significant healing. I gained a deeper understanding of whom and why I was the person I'd become. Better yet, I gained acceptance of myself. I wrote poetry again, which I hadn't done for many years. I had forgotten that I even knew how to write poems! My innocence started to come back as I reclaimed that part of myself.

Two "stretches" absolutely changed my life. The first one involved attending a large annual fair, in the heart of Boise City. Thousands of people gathered in the park to celebrate the annual jazz festival. My task was to dress in the most unattractive, dorkiest clothes I could round up at the Salvation Army and go to the fair.

There, I had to locate the best-looking man I could find. The requirement was that he had to be drop-dead gorgeous. Once I had found him, my mission was to approach and serenade him with "You Are So Beautiful."

I went to the fair wearing hideous plaid polyester pants and a clashing purple shirt. I wasn't even allowed to wear makeup or fix my hair. My eyes were swollen from crying all night the night before, as I did every night while I was at training.

I wasn't happy with my assignment. I felt like a complete fool dressed the way I was, looking terrible and I had no desire to sing to a total stranger. I couldn't even carry a simple tune and this type of exercise went well beyond my comfort level. But I was determined to go through with it.

I sat in the park with two people whose role was to support me. Later I would support them during their stretches. Self-conscious of my dorky clothes, I looked around at the sea of people. Couples walked by arm in arm. Giggling children ran past me. Moms and dads pushed strollers along. Suddenly, I spotted him—the most handsome man in the park. My heart skipped a beat, not because he was attractive, but because now I had to complete my mission.

He was sitting alone on a bench, and all around him were throngs of people enjoying the fair. I took a deep breath, walked over to him, sat down, and said hi. He looked up and recoiled.

He didn't return my greeting. I could tell he was thinking, What a freak! I started to feel panicky but I told myself it was now or never. Mustering every ounce of courage left in me, I looked straight at him and asked, "Can I sing a song for you?"

"Yeah, whatever," he chuckled.

"You are so beautiful to me . . . ." My voice cracked, and I was way off key. I was completely focused on staying composed and holding back my tears.

Then he laughed at me, and I couldn't hold back the tears any longer. I started to cry, but through the tears I kept singing. "You are so beautiful, to me, can't you see?" I kept crying and singing and he kept laughing.

I stopped caring, just kept singing that stupid song.

He finally stopped laughing long enough to take a good look at me, and the moment our eyes met, he began to cry as well. I was stunned. When I finished singing, he stood up and gave me a big hug.

"I've never seen anybody do that before," he said. "I'm sorry I laughed at you. That was incredible. I want you to meet my wife." He hurried off to find her.

But my job was done. I left and went to support my companions during hours it took them to work through their stretches.

Toward the end of the afternoon, from the busyness of the crowd, my gorgeous man materialized with a woman and a little girl. He walked over to me and hugged me again, and then he introduced me to his wife and daughter. He thanked me for being real and for not worrying about what others might think.

That afternoon, with the help of a stranger, I learned a very valuable lesson: It was okay to be me, no matter what I looked like on the outside. If I were just myself, people would respond genuinely, regardless of how I looked.

I had to learn this important lesson because all along my focus had been in the wrong place. I always made sure that when I left the house, I was impeccable: makeup on, perfect hair, sexy clothes.

My first "stretch" of the second training taught me that I could be the ugliest thing you ever saw, and people could still like me. I didn't have to be a sexual object. I could just be me.

From that point on, I changed. The clothes I wore, the way I fixed my hair, the way I acted with people . . . everything changed. I stopped being a hideous flirt. I stopped wearing ultra-short skirts and super tight tops to work. I started wearing suits that made me look more professional to work and on weekends I wore Levis, T-shirts, and tennis shoes instead of short shorts and halter-tops. I looked pretty, but I no longer looked like a whore.

The second stretch that transformed my life had to do with my faith in God. When it came to God, I had become a defiant person. I was so pissed off about my life that I had reached the point of not believing in God. Thankfully, during Level II I started talking to God again all the time like I had most of my life. In level one I wrote to God in my journal for the first time in years but this was different. It was to say hi and not to complain. I used to share everything with God and now I was again.

I still worried that God had stopped listening to me, so I asked Him to give me a concrete sign that proved He was there for me. God came through loud and clear during (and after) my Level II final stretch. My task was to perform a skit where I went from being a caterpillar to blossoming into a beautiful butterfly. I had to go all out with this, making my own costume and finding music to accompany my skit. It seemed like a silly exercise, but I took it seriously. I made my butterfly costume and put my heart into acting out the scene.

Others were doing skits, too. During one of our breaks, in between people's performances, I received a phone message from Nancy's kindergarten teacher. She was extremely upset and wanted to see me the minute I got home, even before our scheduled parent-teacher conference. *What could have made her so upset?* I saved the phone message and mentally put it aside for the time being. After a couple more people performed, it was time for me to get on stage.

During my performance, something amazing happened: I felt like I was having an out-of-body experience. From above, I watched myself transform into a butterfly. I watched my body dance and observed the people watching me. As amazing as this felt, what happened next floored me. It's hard to put into words, but I felt, with every fiber of my being, that I was standing right next to God.

I saw this incredible white light, and it engulfed me. I could feel the warmth of someone holding me close. It was not like a hug, but an intensity that pierced me. Everything tingled and I no longer felt like I was part of this world. Together we were watching me dance.

Nancy

It was an absolutely beautiful experience. Talk about confirmation!

Training came to a close, and I returned home. I had so much to process and comprehend. But before tackling anything else, I had to meet with Nancy's kindergarten teacher first thing on Monday morning.

I walked into the classroom, and the teacher was absolutely beside herself. She went on about how Nancy refused to do what she was told and how she was defiant with her. She was yelling about Nancy being completely out of control. She kept walking in a circle saying she did it wrong, wrong, wrong, and yelling at me to do something about it. Her being so upset worried me.

She finally calmed down and sat at the desk with me. Then she explained that she had asked the class to draw pictures of their parents. She showed me Nancy's drawing of her dad. It was cute, what you'd expect a five year old to draw. Then the teacher pulled out the picture Nancy drew of me, and my jaw dropped to the floor.

It was a picture of a butterfly. Even though Nancy had absolutely no knowledge of my butterfly skit, she had drawn me, as I was when I reconnected with God.

I just sat there and bawled. The teacher was upset and on the verge of tears because her student drew a butterfly instead of a person. I cried tears of joy, thankful for this miracle that came from my intuitive child. She had drawn everything perfectly; her butterfly had the same colors, even the same polka dots, my costume had, yet she had never seen my costume. Here was even more confirmation from God. What more did I need?

I looked into the teacher's eyes. "Sometimes, things look different than we expect them to," I began. "Please, can you allow Nancy to have this picture? This is how she sees me, and I think it's beautiful."

From that moment on, my connection with God grew, becoming the way it had been when I was a child only stronger now. My relationship with my kids changed, too. I could feel all my love for them again. I was able to take a good look at them, and tell them I was sorry. I could tell them that I regretted missing so much of their lives. I assured them that things would be different, and that now I could be there for them.

Each child reacted differently. All of them were scared, because suddenly I was a very different person. Shawn cried. He couldn't believe that I could actually talk to him face to face. He wasn't used to having a mother who stood up and defended herself. Wendy was shocked that I could actually speak with confidence. Katy shut down and distanced herself further. I asked her to look in my eyes so I could tell her how sorry I was, but she wouldn't. She closed her eyes and walked away.

Only Nancy was fine with the "new me." She simply said, "OK, Mommy, I love you." But the older kids were terrified. They knew something was brewing, and they felt their security threatened.

But their feelings of insecurity paled compared to what Joe was going through. He tried to insult and criticize me, but I stopped him.

"Don't insult me," I said firmly. "I'm not going to accept it anymore. I don't like it. You don't get to talk to me that way ever again." His world was turning upside down, and he didn't know how to deal with it.

Once again, he resorted to drinking heavily. He also started doing something I hadn't seen him do before: he frequently slumped down on the couch and sobbed uncontrollably. Joe begged me to stay home and not go through with the third level of training. He didn't like the person I was becoming. Emotionally, he was a complete wreck. I was not. For the first time in my adult life I felt alive. I actually liked being me.

Joe threatened suicide a few times. One evening he got completely drunk and went into our garage, held a shotgun to his head, and said, "I'm through."

Standing at the doorway crying, I told him, "This isn't the answer! There's got to be a better way to live, Joe." Then I rushed back to the kitchen and called 911.

Joe followed me into the house. I was scared to death; afraid he'd either kill himself or turn the gun against me. I shook with the fear of his actions and imbalance. He saw me call the police and became angry. Not wanting to face the police, he forced me to get into the car with him. He left his shotgun in the garage, and we drove around the neighborhood for a long time.

When we finally went back home, the police were there. The officers confronted Joe, telling him that if he didn't enroll in some kind of counseling, they would lock him up. They told him he was a menace, not only to me, and the kids, to the entire neighborhood. Joe was cornered. He had to agree; otherwise he faced jail, and possibly prison. He grudgingly went to counseling, and made the decision that he was going to try the training too. He made it through level one, but at the beginning of the second level he quit.

I focused on getting whole. A door that had been closed since I was a child had finally opened for me. I started to hear angels singing again. I heard my familiar dad talk to me more, especially during quiet moments such as when I was cleaning my house. His soothing voice clearly offered comforting words like, "Hi there, it's been awhile. Are you ready to listen?"

I was.

Dad was bringing me messages from God, not just as spoken words but they also were coming in through different venues. Sometimes my father's voice carried them. Other times, I'd get signs from things I'd find. I found three pennies in the laundry room. They were situated as if someone had placed them there. I didn't pay much attention to them but I went to the store shortly after and when I was waiting in line the checker was telling the girl in front of me how it was a sign from the other side. She said if you find coins placed oddly, it usually is three pennies. Then I started finding three pennies everywhere. I found them in the bathroom on the floor. I found them on the bumper of my car, in the girls' room on the floor, in the kitchen drawer and every morning in our laundry room for a month.

I would also find mysterious notes left throughout the house. Old notes from Dad, silly ones, would show up on my bathroom counter, or just lying on the floor. I found birthday cards he wrote to me from years before. These notes and cards were all in my hope chest and some of them I had never seen before. I found things like his cufflinks on the floor in my room when I knew they were in my jewelry box.

Things got even stranger. I would hear him call my name and then the T.V. would turn on. I would turn it off and it would come right back on. Then the appliances in the kitchen would take turns turning on. I didn't know how these events happened, but I accepted them. I felt comforted to know that I was receiving help from the other side. This made me even more secure with myself I knew I was not alone and never would be. I still poured my heart into my work but I had to pull back for a while. I needed to focus on the end of the training. The third and last level of training was a break through. I knew in my heart my marriage could not be saved. There was nothing to save! I knew I was no longer in love with my husband; I loved him, but could never be in love with him again. I knew that I wanted to dance for the rest of my life even if that meant dancing alone. I knew I never stopped loving my mother and wanted to be with her more than I ever had in my life. I wanted to know her. I knew that I would show my children a better way to live even if it was the last thing I ever did on this earth. Most importantly I was starting to know me!

13

FORGIVENESS
1996–1998

When you hold resentment toward another,
You are bound to that person or condition
By an emotional link that is stronger than steel.
Forgiveness is the only way
To dissolve that link
And get free.
—Catherine Ponder

My four and a half months of specialized training with Spectrum were more powerful and transforming than any other period of my life. The training facilitators helped me be aware of my emotional baggage. I let go of baggage I didn't know I'd been carrying. After they had worked with me through my childhood rape, I truly was transformed at every level. I stopped feeling physically sick. I stopped vomiting every time I thought about my uncle. I started to feel whole again.

During my very first day of training, I had shared with the group what an awful person I'd become. My introduction went something like this: "Hi, my name's Debbie. I am a whore. I am a slut. I have had so many affairs. I've cheated on my husband for years. I am a liar. I'm not worthy of anything. I'm not trustworthy; you can't trust me. This is who I am."

I remember the looks I got after I had said those words. Thirty people stared at me in total shock. Even my facilitator had a look of alarm. I kept going. I went into horrid detail about how I had lied, stolen Joe's money, and cheated on him for the last four years of our marriage. Of course, he'd done the same, and worse, to me, but I didn't go there. This was about me, and this was how I felt. Despite all those stares, I was glad to get it out into the open. It felt so good to confess my secrets, to get them off my chest, and to just own that this is who I had become.

Despite my shocking introduction, my facilitator and all my future facilitators did not back off. They treated me with dignity. As other details of my life emerged, from my broken childhood to my broken marriage, their compassion toward me grew. In their eyes, I was not the whore I had presented to them. To them, I was a broken spirit in need of healing.

They helped me arrive at major revelations that ultimately restored who I was. My first revelation—that I had become just like my mother–taught me that I didn't hate every aspect of my mom. But what I did hate about her was exactly what I had become, such as having affairs and the way I treated my children and therefore what I also hated in me. I had made the same choices she made and ended up like her. This realization was the beginning of my healing transformation.

My second huge revelation was that somewhere along the way, I'd lost my true self. *Where had I gone? At what point had I lost sight of my babies?* I was so out of touch with them. *What was going on in their lives, their minds, and their hearts?* I realized that I missed my children deeply, and that I had missed being an integral part of their lives. When I reached that realization, all I wanted to do was run home and hold my kids forever. Suddenly, I was able to feel my children's love completely again, along with my own love for them and I felt restored.

When I did get home and saw my kids, a flood of emotions hit me. I ran to them and gave each a hug, which took them by surprise. I told them how sorry I was for having been gone so long. They got hit with a flood of emotions as well. They were happy but scared. They were distrustful yet hopeful. Guardedly, they watched me. *Was this for real? Was Mom truly going to change?* It was the start of a long healing process between my children and me.

There was also a revelation that part of me had never really grown up. I clearly remember the day my facilitator said, "You've been nine years old all your life." That hit me hard. When my uncle raped me and threatened me to keep quiet, something inside my soul got stuck. Part of me stopped growing. Now I had a choice: quit this process I'd begun and go home, or grow up. I chose to grow up.

The training facilitators helped me and all the other trainees grow up. To my surprise, I found this part fun. The process began with each of us taking the little child that we still were and embracing that child. I hugged the child, rocked the child, and told her how sorry I was that I had let her down. I told her I was sorry I had abandoned her, and then I played and danced with her. The process of embracing this child took two days.

What followed were the "stretches," and then our life-altering skits, where I underwent my transformation from caterpillar to butterfly. That's how I started my "grown up life," in a very beautiful way.

It was a celebration, with God giving me back all of my light at that one particular moment in time. My spiritual being came back during my butterfly skit; incredibly, the others in the room saw it, too. My facilitators told me they'd never before seen anybody go through such a powerful transformation back to the light the way I had. They said they knew God was in the room. What a special gift I'd been given.

During those four and a half months, I changed from somebody that I hated into my true self. At my graduation, I stood before my fellow graduates, the facilitators, and my children (I was so happy and proud to have them there), and most importantly Joe, and I introduced myself again. This time, I stood proudly and with confidence, honesty, and honor, I simply said, "I am a free, trustworthy, loving woman. My name is Debbie." I felt something inside me like I had never felt before—I believed in myself. I knew I was ok and that this would grow. To this day, I display those powerful words at home up on the wall in my room.

This is when my life began. This is when my dreams started. The adventure had just begun.

During the past several months, I had been accountable for my life and where I was. I was ready for a change. We agreed to not change anything big in our lives for the first ninety days after we graduated the training. I sat on the porch with a cup of coffee and told Joe that when my ninety days was up, I was leaving. He laughed and said he'd heard that before. He was sure that this would pass in a couple of weeks and everything would go back to the way it had always been. But what I saw in his eyes told a very different story. He didn't believe his own words—he knew that I would really leave this time.

It was two weeks after the training when Sarah went into labor. We waited in the waiting room for the news. It was one of the most beautiful moments in my life when Shawn came out of the delivery room with his baby tucked tight against him. He ran to me, and hugged me, sobbing, when he told me he was finally a daddy. Shawn and Sarah had a beautiful baby girl.

I was a grandma! I was even more determined to make life better. I wanted my son to be a good father and a good husband to his wife. When I held my granddaughter, Hokulealani, for the first time, I cried. I spent as much time as I could with Sarah and the baby during the next several weeks. The rest of my time, I spent with the girls. We went shopping for summer clothes and we went hiking in the mountains. I took them places we had never been

Shawn and Hokulealani

before. We even went on a four-day trip to Zions National Park and stayed in a luxury hotel there. When we returned home, I spent three days shopping with Wendy for a wedding dress.

Then the day finally arrived when I could make major changes in my life. It was 4:30 PM and I was on the front porch waiting for Joe to return home from work. I had the car loaded with my clothes and I was ready. When Joe pulled into the driveway he knew. He got out of his truck, came over to the porch, sat down and said nothing. I looked at him and said, "This is it—it's time for me to go." I put the girls in the car and I left. I had put an apartment on hold two weeks prior so that I knew I had a place to go.

The next year of my life was a living hell. My children wouldn't speak to me, convinced that I had ruined their lives. Nothing would ever be the same. I stood strong. Wendy's wedding came and went and it was beautiful. The tension was horrible, but we did it.

From there life got much harder, Shawn would call and scream at me, telling me that if I wanted to be part of his baby's life I had to go home and stop this. The thought of not being part of my granddaughter's life terrified me. I started to doubt myself, so I went back to counseling to help me stay strong. My counselor urged me to let Katy stay with her father because she was in junior high and needed to be near her friends. She said Katy would never make it if I didn't.

Katy and Nancy

I was falling apart, and my work also started to suffer. I spent all my time desperately trying to cope with my children. Nancy was in a new elementary school and hated the apartment. Katy was now back at home with her father who spent all of his time drinking and telling her it was my fault. Shawn's phone calls came at all hours of the night yelling and screaming for me to go home. And Wendy, now married, would not talk to me and made it very clear she wanted nothing to do with me.

I was losing my grip, I knew the counselor was wrong about leaving Katy and I realized I had created a mess. I left her with her father scared and confused. Nancy was crying herself to sleep every night and refused to go to school. Katy called me all night until I agreed to go pick her up and let her sleep over. Work continued to get worse because I wasn't answering my calls and I couldn't deal with the stress at the office on top of the stress at home. I was falling apart. I was scared and all alone.

Three months went by like this and I lost two major accounts. I had also started drinking again. Katy was with Nancy and me most of the time, and not going to school. Nancy wasn't going to school either. We spent our days in that small apartment together, mostly crying. I was drinking myself stupid, convinced that I had made the most awful mistake I had ever made in my life. Gary dropped by to check on me and was furious to find me in the state I was. He pleaded with me to pull my head out of the ground.

Still I plummeted downward—I could not bear being without my kids. Having them hate me was the worst pain I had to ever deal with. Then one weekend Nancy went to her father's house to spend the night. He usually never took her but his dad was up from California to see the kids. When Nancy came home, she was clearly upset and told me she wasn't supposed to love me anymore. I questioned her further and she explained that her grandpa said I was no longer a part of the family and that she should treat me that way. Joe told all of them that I was in love with Gary and that was why I had left him. I was so angry I could hardly breathe. He also told them that loyalty meant staying together and I wasn't loyal.

I got the girls ready for bed, read to them, and cried in the dark by myself. I was ashamed of my father in law and ashamed of my husband. *How could they hurt my children this way? What had I done, my moment of truth and weakness to lead to this?* I knew I wasn't in love with Gary after the training, I knew I was in love with a friendship. I wasn't capable of loving anyone then—including myself. I had no idea Joe would use my moment of weakness against me in the worst way, with my children. I hated him! And I hated his father.

I continued to drink and not go to work and before long I was completely broke. My rent was a month late and we had no food in the house. I went to Gary and asked him to loan me rent money with the promise I would pay it back. He said yes without hesitation and told me to get back to work. He also asked me how things were going and I fell apart. I explained what happened with the kids and

Joe. When I was done, he smiled and told me it would be okay. He said that my kids would someday understand the truth and even if they didn't—he and I knew. He wrote me a check for my rent and I left. I knew he still believed in me, no matter how bad things looked at the moment.

The next day, after getting Nancy and Katy to school, I went back to work. It wasn't a good thing. I had made a mess of my accounts and my clients were not going to be so forgiving. I had to start over and I knew it. That night, when I picked up the girls to go home I knew they were going to be hungry. I had put my last five dollars in the gas tank and was not sure what to do for dinner. I felt like giving up. But, when we got home and stopped by the office to pay the rent, the manager told me that there was a huge pile of groceries waiting for us. I didn't understand what she was saying. She told me some guy had brought in the groceries and asked her not to tell me. When I asked her his name she said he wouldn't say. At first I thought it was Joe in another attempt to control me. But the manager told me what a sweet guy he was. I asked her what he looked like and realized it was Gary. I took the groceries and went home with my girls. It was time to make this work. It was time to get my life in order.

I got up the next morning and got the girls up and ready for school. After dropping Katy off, I took Nancy to school where she cried and refused to leave the car. After sitting in the car for thirty minutes pleading with Nancy to get out, someone knocked on the car window. I looked up and the principal was standing there. I rolled the window down and the principal, with a big smile, asked if we would come in his office to talk. Nancy and I followed him in. He sent Nancy into the cafeteria for breakfast with his secretary and then closed the door. You can't imagine the trouble I expected. Instead, he started to explain to me that four years ago he and his wife divorced. He also told me that he started drinking after the divorce to deal with the pain and almost lost everything. When he showed up in court at a custody hearing it was clear to the judge he was drunk and he lost visitation rights and was ordered to under go rehab before he was able to see his kids again. *What did that have to do with me?* He had been watching Nancy and me for the last six months every morning. He knew I was drinking and was separated and he wanted to help. After two hours of talking, he promised to be there for us both on bad mornings to help me avoid the same mistakes he had made. We made an agreement, he hugged me and I left the school with another angel in my life.

I stopped drinking and started to put my life back together. It wasn't easy but I found new accounts and eventually paid the rent loan back to Gary. Neither of us ever mentioned the groceries and to this day still haven't. I worked hard and kept going, hoping someday my two oldest children would understand why I had left. With many confrontations and heartaches I continued on my path, believing in myself. However, in order for me to truly make it in the world, I had something else to repair. I needed to call my mom. I knew I had to forgive her. I didn't know what forgiveness meant or involved exactly, but I knew that without forgiveness, I'd remain stuck. I decided that the first step was to go to counseling. Not just by myself, but with my mom. She was sixty-one, I was forty-one, and finally I was ready to make amends with her.

This time when I let my Mom back into my life, it was forever. She showed up at my apartment unexpectedly. I invited her in and told her about moving out. She said she was proud of me and she knew what a difficult time this was and how it would probably get harder before it got better.

I asked her about going to counseling together. I had a lot of things I needed to say to her and that I thought a go-between would be good. The truth was, I feared telling Mom how I had felt about her for so long.

Yet, she was excited and told me we could go to her counselor. She had an appointment the following week and would let her counselor know that I would be joining her. The day came and I was there early and nervous.

I had waited a long time to let my Mom be part of my life and now I just wanted her to love me. Most of all I wanted to love her. When we walked in together I looked over at my Mom and she was crying; her tears took me by surprise.

"Mom, what's wrong?"

"I'm scared, Debbie."

"Why?"

"What if you decide that you don't like me?"

I grabbed her in my arms. "Mom, I am so sorry for all of this. You are always a part of me; you always will be. For so long, I've missed you."

Then the counselor, with a big smile, intervened, "Well then, let's get started!"

During our therapy, I learned about Mom's childhood. I had never known that she had been abused. As the words poured out of her, I felt love pour out of my heart for her. I realized she never wanted to hurt me. All along, she just wanted to help and protect me. My love for her overflowed.

The counselor held out a red notebook to me. When I looked at Mom for an explanation, she was fighting back tears. I could see the fear in her eyes.

"These are your Mom's journals about her father and the abuse she has endured. Are you strong enough to read them?" the counselor queried.

I felt nauseous, but when Mom smiled at me, I knew I could read them. I opened the first group of pages in the red journal and began to read to myself. I made it through the first three chapters and was crying uncontrollably.

"Debbie," the counselor asked, "Do you need a break?"

"Yes, I do." I tried breathing deeply.

We changed the subject and talked about me leaving Joe and how the separation and moving out of my home was affecting me. After that, I once again, walked through the abuse I had experienced at the hands of my uncle. Once again it was painful . . . but cathartic. When I finished, it was time to go the distance . . . to release all the anger I had held towards my mother. I told her that for decades I had blamed her, because when I was a little girl she had sent me back to my uncle's place against my wishes. As my anger surfaced, I didn't hold back. I told my mother it was her fault. I said that I had always believed that she hated me.

Mom just sat there and listened quietly. When I was finally through, I looked at her and felt a tremendous awe for her strength. She let me get every last, ugly bit out, and throughout my dumping and my anger, she sat there with dignity, emanating love for me. She didn't say a word. She let me vent and never wavered in her love for me.

Our counseling session went on for three and a half hours. Emotionally, we were exhausted. Yet, our insightful therapist knew we were making incredible headway, so she kept us in that room; clearing the stormy past until both of us were freer.

Once we had cleared all the anger and the pain, Mom and I were able to talk, face to face, heart to heart. I finally told her that I missed her and I loved her. That moment was our final breakthrough, allowing our relationship the healing we needed.

It took me four sessions to get through Mom's journals of her father's abuse. She wrote about hiding behind the stove and asking God not to let her father find her. It broke my heart! I was in shock and could not believe my mother had survived this horrible abuse. We went to counseling together for six months every other week. Not only did we go through Mom's journals, but she shared for the first time all about her work with her foster kids and why they meant so much to her.

I grew to respect my mother unlike any other person I had ever met. She was a very powerful and beautiful person. She was a survivor and never again would I see my mother as less than beautiful. Her strength inspired me.

After each visit to the counselor's, Mom and I would go out for coffee. Then we would go back to my house and stay up talking and laughing all night. We had lost so much time and had a lot of catching up to do. I loved my mom, and I never wanted to push her out of my life again. Thankfully, I never did. From that point on, she was in my life to stay.

Before leaving the therapist's office for the final time, Mom shared her notes about our counseling together. She wrote how grateful she was that I let her into my life. She wrote about my growth and how she was so thrilled that I was ready to confront my uncle. In her final passage, she wrote:

Dear God thank you for everything. Thank you for bringing my daughter back to me. I have missed her for a long time.

The last thing Mom and I discussed in counseling were dreams. She brought up the topic by asking me what my dreams were. I looked at her, gave a little chuckle, and said, "I'm too old for that."

"I don't ever want to hear you say that again."

"What do you mean, Mom?"

"That you're too old. You're not old until your dreams aren't dreams anymore. When you stop dreaming, you are old." Mom urged me to go after my dreams.

Three months later, I was ready for my next step of facing my biggest monster. I knew that if I didn't confront my uncle while I had the courage, the rape would haunt me forever and prevent me from reaching my dreams. I didn't want any more obstacles in my way.

I picked up the phone and called Mom.

"Mom, I'm ready. Let's do it."

"What are we doing?" she asked.

"We're going to talk with my uncle."

I could hear her take a big, deep breath and then release it with a deep sigh. Then silence.

Mom and me

After a few moments, Mom asked, "Okay, our big adventure. When are we going?"

"I'll set an appointment with him for the following week."

"No, Debbie. Let's not wait a whole week. Let's do it as quickly as we can."

"Okay Mom, I'll see what I can arrange in the next several days."

By now, my uncle was fifty-four years old. I didn't know the man. I hadn't spoken a single word to him since I was nine years old. At family reunions he always tried to say hello to me, but I simply turned around and walked away.

Now I was picking up the phone and calling him. My hands were shaking. I could tell he was surprised to hear my voice. "I need to see you," I told him. By his silence, I presumed he knew what I wanted to talk about. I told him where we'd meet and at what time. "I'll be there," he said.

Mom and I went to the restaurant together. I looked at her and noticed how stiffly she sat. Her arms hugged her abdomen. She was as scared as I was. For the first time in my life, I could see in her face all the hurt and pain she felt at what he had done to her little girl. I'd never seen that before and it was an enlightening experience.

We arrived before my uncle did. When he walked into the restaurant, I could feel my whole body want to get up and leave. I actually had to hold my legs down to keep myself from running off. I was scared to death. I didn't want to walk through that final door, the door I had kept closed for most of my life. I didn't want to face the monster. But my dreams depended on it. With my mother by my side, I summoned the courage to go through with this meeting.

As the three of us sat at the table, I said, "We're gonna start with all my memories. This is what I remember." I walked my uncle through everything. I told him in detail what I remembered and how I had felt. As I spoke, it was difficult to look at him. He didn't look like the evil-peddler who had raped me. He looked like a scared little boy. Then something happened that I never would have imagined in a million years: my heart opened up to him. I felt his pain.

I watched this man whom I barely knew sob.

"I've hated you all my life since you hurt me," I told him. "I trusted you. You were my friend, my uncle, my family. You destroyed my marriage. You destroyed me." I did not hold back. With my mother next to me as a silent witness crying softly and holding my hand, I told him everything.

As these words left my mouth, I saw the pain I'd carried for years leave my body and go back into him. I saw him absorb all of it, and for a moment I worried he'd have a heart attack because he looked awful. He became terribly pale; he looked like he was dying. I could feel how badly he was hurting.

My uncle cried for a long time without saying a word. He couldn't stop crying. Through the tears, he repeated over and over again, "God, I'm sorry. I'm so sorry. What have I done? Oh my God, what have I done?"

I told him, "You get to keep it now. It's yours."

We were done. I stood up, and so did Mom. My uncle also stood up and as I looked at him, I was taken aback at how small and frail he appeared. My heart went out to him. I walked over to him and gave him a hug.

He wasn't a monster to me anymore. Instead, he became a little person who had made a horrible mistake. I forgave him. I didn't have to ask God anymore how to forgive. I finally knew how.

The hurt went away. The pain I had carried from the time I was nine years old finally disappeared. What's more, I could face my uncle again and see an actual human being. If I ran into him at the store, I no longer turned around and rushed off. I was able to say hello and even give him a heartfelt hug. Whenever I hugged him, I could feel his pain. I know he'll carry it with him for the rest of his life. But it wasn't mine anymore, and I'm really glad about that. I was finally free.

I learned a lot about forgiveness. Before, I had no idea how to go about forgiving someone who had hurt me so badly. But when I finally saw the humanity in the one who had hurt me, it was easy.

Forgiveness feels good. Once you have forgiveness in your heart, you can feel God, and God feels like a huge amount of light, an almost unbearable measure of joy. I just wanted to get on my knees and take everything in. I felt as if I was *feeling* for the first time in my life. I felt overwhelmed by all the love I had to give to others.

It was like being elevated to some place that's not on this earth. I was here, but I was connected to something bigger. It was like transcending the fears and the pain here and walking in the world, yet not being in it. In short, it was amazing.

That ugly dark spot of fear, anger, and resentment that had been eating away at my body and soul turned into pure love. Horrid people merely turned into little lost spirits. With forgiveness in my heart, I was able to see right into them and love them. It was weird, but incredible: I felt their horrible pain, and I was able to love them without loving what they'd done. When I could connect to their souls, I could see who they really were beyond their choices and actions.

It was important for me to share all of this with my children. I wanted them to know the power of forgiveness. So over time, as they were ready, I told them, one by one, the whole story about my uncle. They'd already heard the rumors, so they knew some "event" had occurred. I wanted to tell them exactly what had taken place, because half-truths confuse, but complete truth empowers.

My girls wanted to know how I could speak to my uncle and how I could hug him. I continued to explain forgiveness to them as best I could. Wendy reached the point where she understood the power of forgiveness. My two younger girls are still processing what it all means.

My life was falling into place, finally at my age of forty-one. My fear of my uncle was gone, my relationship with my Mom had bloomed and I was working on being back in my kids' lives. I was on my way to making it!

There was only one part left to deal with: my marriage. During Spectrum training, I remembered how much I loved Joe. I remembered how, at age sixteen, I enjoyed being pregnant with his child, and completely in love with him. I reviewed and relived the wonderful newness of being a kid in love, starting my life with the man of my dreams. That love lifted me up.

I remembered when I graduated from Spectrum, one of my facilitators asked me, "What are you going to do now with all this new knowledge you have of yourself? You're a beautiful woman. You have all your light back. You have all your love. Your kids are right here with you. What are you going to do?"

Beaming, I said, "I'm going back home and fix my marriage. I love him so much. I'm going to make it work." She looked disappointed. I could tell she felt we were right back at square one.

She replied, "Well, you go right ahead. You just keep dancing that dance. You just don't get it, do you?" I didn't understand why she was mad at me. However, she was right, I didn't get it.

Once I was headed back home, I started to comprehend what she was trying to tell me. I knew darn well that Joe didn't love me and couldn't love me, but I was going to keep deceiving myself. I was going to keep dancing, thinking my life with Joe would magically turn into happily ever after. I was still hanging on to my fairy tale and my commitment I shared with Grandma so long ago.

For the first time, after moving out and taking back my life, I could clearly see that Joe did not love me. My kids were able to respond to my love. My husband was not.

It was over. I had made the decision to leave and now it was time to end my marriage for good. I told Joe I was ready to sign the divorce papers. Even though I had already moved out of our home it was the hardest thing I'd ever done, even harder than meeting with my uncle. But I didn't cry. It didn't hurt. I simply looked up at the sky and said to myself, "There. I've taken off my dancing shoes."

14

TIME FOR DIVORCE
1998

It may take time to develop your core heart potential, but as you uncover a deeper connection with the power of the heart, you'll find more appreciation, love, and forgiveness at its core. New freedom will come as you clean out old mind-sets, hurts, pains, and resistances.
—Doc Childre and Howard Martin, *The HeartMath Solution*

One step at a time, to a new life . . . The act of leaving Joe was empowering, terrifying, and heartbreaking all at the same time. I had never lived by myself. As a teen I had gone straight from my parent's house to living with Joe. At age forty-one, I didn't have a clue what it was like to be on my own and I was terrified.

On the other hand, I experienced a lightness and freedom. I wanted to jump on the bed and act like a kid. Emotions played tug-of-war with my heart, one minute feeling great, the next minute panicking and asking myself, Now what have I done? Am I going to be okay?

Could my happiness really last? This is the ultimate question that all abused women and wives might ask: *Is my happiness real and lasting?*

I replayed the afternoon I stood on the front porch and announced that I was leaving. I replayed everything that took place up to where I was now.

I thought about all the threatening calls Joe had made in the first few months after moving out—the times I almost gave up after being out of work with no food in the house and no rent money. I could handle it all except the heartbreak of being at odds with my kids.

There were times when I seriously considered going back. I worried that by leaving I had destroyed my children completely. That was a horrible feeling. On so many levels I had hurt my kids, and I saw no forgiveness in sight.

I had hit rock bottom by drinking and losing the work I had poured my heart into.

I remembered the school principal knocking on the car window and me looking back through tear soaked eyes. How he gave so much to a woman and child he didn't know.

I also replayed the phone calls to and from Evan. Evan was my buddy in Spectrum. I remembered the first time I met her we were suppose to say what we thought, I told her she was beautiful. Evan's reply was "what are you, fu—ing nuts?" A very unlikely pair, she and I, we ended up with a close friendship and stayed that way. After spectrum we would call each other two to four times a week. Then it slowed down to once a week. Evan divorced a week before I moved out and we would share everything over the phone together. We would laugh for hours making fun of each other, even in our darkest moments. We had a strange connection indeed. Nancy was missing one afternoon and I was running through the neighborhood searching franticly. After I found her, we returned home and I was still upset. The phone was ringing when I answered it, and Evan was on the other line wondering where Nancy was. When I told Evan I had found her down the street, she told me to give her a hug and said goodbye. The thing is, I hadn't called Evan when I couldn't find Nancy and neither had anyone else. I never questioned how she knew, it had happened to us before and we both understood it. Evan was my strength so much of the time, and I was hers. We would laugh off the hurt by telling each other how we would be rich some-day and happily married to our Prince Charmings. Evan is a gift of friendship and love. She is and will always be my sister.

I also remembered the morning Gary showed up at the apart-ment looking for me. "You need to pull it together," Gary told me. "You're losing it. You're a disaster. Where's Nancy? You're going to lose that little girl. After you have fought so hard to keep her. What are you doing? Get off your ass. Comb your hair. Get back to work."

Then he was gone. I remembered the rent money he had loaned me—and the mysterious groceries.

I remembered stopping by the shop one afternoon shortly after I went back to work, Gary had a huge grin on his face, because he knew I was okay and I was going to make it.

I thought about how, throughout all of this, Joe continued to poison our kids against me. How he fed them a steady stream of lies designed to alienate them from me. And I remembered his phone calls asking me if we were hungry enough yet, if I was through play-ing this ridiculous game. And the threats he made to take Nancy, constantly telling me to bring Nancy home because I couldn't take care of her. He never wanted to take care of her, but he wanted to hurt me. He used my kids without consideration to whether or not he was hurting them. It was just a way to get to me.

I remembered the confrontations Shawn had with Gary, accus-ing him of having an affair with me. Gary stood strong, knowing he didn't owe anybody an explanation. In time, he figured, they would see the truth.

I remembered how he told my son, "I love your mother. She's my friend, and that is all you're ever going to hear."

I had asked Gary why he didn't stand up for himself. He replied,

"I know what I've done. I know who I am. I don't owe Shawn or your ex-husband or anyone else an explanation. I have done nothing that deserves an explanation except love a very good friend. I'll stand by that for the rest of my life."

I had relived everything up until this moment and now it was time. It was time to divorce, time to move forward, it was time to live!

Joe and I had been separated four months when he started divorce proceedings. He hired an attorney and they drafted the papers. Joe called me and said, "I want you to just sign the papers. Let's just get this over with."

It had been six months since I had moved out. I was ready to sign the papers.

Joe and I met with his attorney. That was a mistake on my part; I should have hired my own attorney. I ended up signing practically everything over to Joe, but I really didn't care. I just wanted him out of my life. The papers went through, and we were divorced. That was it. It was over.

Driving home I thought about Katy—how I had left her, still twelve, living with her dad, how she was with me every weekend and only a few times during the week. I watched my sweet child decline. Little by little, she was losing the sparkle from her eyes. Her face became withdrawn, and she looked empty.

By herself, she often came to my place in the middle of the week because she couldn't stand to be around her father's negative energy. She even stopped going to school. My resilient fighter had lost her spirit and cried all the time. *What had I done?* I felt I had abandoned Katy and I also had to be the one to rescue her. I had to bring her home with me for good.

I was doing well enough now we could move out of the apartment and find someplace with a room for the girls. While searching for a larger home, I found a small house that was large enough for the three of us. It had a full basement with its own kitchen and entry. I approached Shawn about the idea of sharing the house with us. Sarah and he were having financial difficulty and he agreed. I left the apartment. Nancy, Katy and I moved into the upstairs while Shawn, Sarah and Hokulealani moved downstairs in our new home.

Slowly, I watched my daughter's spirit return. She loved the house and she was so happy to have her own room. Most of all, she was happy to get away from her father's dark surroundings. Katy felt safer with me, and our house became her safe haven. She never even asked if she could go spend a weekend with her dad. She would go for a short time but the pain of being with him was too much for her. It took her a good six months to handle his darkness before she was willing to stay with him again.

Nancy was in yet another elementary school, but this one was working. Her teacher made a strong connection with her and gave her stories she found in the library about kids and divorce. I was taking her to counseling once a week and this was also helping.

Shawn and I were talking again and mending our relationship as best we could. Little by little we started to find some common ground we were ok with. I loved having them there with us because it also gave me a chance to become very close to my granddaughter.

Wendy was still very difficult to reach because she was still angry and would only come to see me once every four to six months. She was going to be my hardest challenge of my kids. I wasn't sure if she would ever let me in her life again.

I continued working. I rebuilt my self-esteem as I rebuilt my business. Gary was my cheerleader. He always had words of encouragement for me. I wanted him to be proud of me; I wanted him to know that I *could* do it on my own. More than anything, I wanted this for myself. The next few months I worked extra hard to succeed.

The day came when Gary asked me to a football game. He was single and now I was single. *Dare we risk our beautiful friendship*

and start dating? We had such a fun time together that afternoon that when Gary dropped me off at home, he asked me if I wanted to go to dinner sometime. Our friendship was precious to both of us. This was risky, but I smiled at him and asked if this was going to be a date. When he said it was, I said yes. That was the beginning of new strange territory for us.

Slowly, cautiously, we decided to move our relationship to the next level. I had never been involved with anyone like Gary before. He treated me with respect because he genuinely cared about me. So this was how it felt to be loved! I felt wonderful. We started bowling together and the time came when Gary invited me to bring the girls over for dinner to his place. I asked the girls and they agreed to go. It turned out to be fun. They swam in his pool and he cooked. He could cook well too! We continued to date and I was happy and enjoying my time with him.

Katy, however, wasn't happy about my new relationship. Now that she had me back, she didn't want to share me with anyone. She was very angry with me for dating Gary. Nancy, on the other hand, thought he was great . . . until her siblings told her otherwise. They convinced her that Gary would be bad for them.

I was walking a thin line again. I was dating my friend, the best friend I'd ever had, and I couldn't be happier. But I had fought so hard to win my children back. I didn't want to lose them again. *Did I have to give up one to keep the other?*

Unfortunately, I had no idea how much anger Shawn still carried with him and I ultimately found out the hard way. Shawn and I had a horrible confrontation over Gary, and I was terrified that it would destroy my relationship with him forever. It took a long time to let it go and I am still not sure Shawn has let it go entirely.

I came to the understanding that children watch both parents, and the one who looks the most hurt gets their support and the other parent gets the blame. When I finally realized what was going on, I was ok. I knew someday Joe would be ok and that only then would my children be able to move on. It was a long road and it still is at times, but I hope they have since then learned that there is no blame in a divorce. Children, even grown children, have a hard time seeing their parents as people. They scramble trying to fix everything and try to bring the family back together. They do this without knowing that the family is more together now then they ever were.

15

CHANGE DIRECTION NOW!
1999

A bodily disease, which we look upon as whole and entire within itself, may, after all, be but a symptom of some ailment in the spiritual past.—Nathaniel Hawthorne

Shawn and I got into a horrible screaming battle about Gary after I came home late one night after spending the evening bowling with him.

"Where were you?" my son demanded. He was interrogating me just like Joe had done for twenty four years. Shawn had been keeping close tabs on me for the past year, and I just couldn't take it anymore.

"How dare you?" I yelled back. "I'm so sick of your crap."

I felt rage course through my body, and I slapped him. He stood there and looked at me for a second. His eyes filled with tears—and then he shoved me.

I toppled over and stumbled down a stair or two.

His wife Sarah stood at the top of the stairs, holding the baby, and watched the entire scene unravel. Together with Shawn, she began to scream at me as I screamed back at them.

With all the commotion, Katy and Nancy came running into

the hallway to see what was happening. When I saw fear in their eyes, I told Shawn and Sarah to leave. I told my son I never wanted to see him again. I called the police and then I drove away with Katy and Nancy in the car. We drove around in circles, with the girls crying and me in a state of shock.

When we returned home, the police were there. They had talked to Shawn and Sarah and my son drove off with his family. I took the girls to a motel just to get away from that house because the memories hurt too badly. I was awake most of the night, thinking about my son, about my granddaughter and trying to come to terms with what had happened. I had a sick feeling in the pit of my stomach. I felt like a total failure. I didn't know how to help Shawn go back to the kind and peaceful person he used to be.

The next day Katy, Nancy, and I returned home. The girls went into their rooms. The moment I walked into that house, I felt dizzy, as though I was in a weird state of depression. I tried to walk, but my leg wouldn't respond. It dragged behind me. My arm felt like it fell out of my shoulder. I was losing control of my body and felt a strange pressure inside my head. What was going on?

I picked up the phone and called Gary. As I talked to him, I noticed that my words were coming out slurred. I had no idea what was wrong. I lay down on the stairs and spent ten minutes trying to move my body. I looked around and wondered, *What the hell happened to me?* Then, I blacked out.

I came to a few minutes later and again wondered what had happened. Was this a result of all the stress I'd gone through the night before? Was I having a nervous breakdown? I stood up and walked to the bathroom. I threw up. I went to bed and fell asleep.

The next morning I woke up and was relieved to find my body had gone back to feeling normal. I still felt sick and awful about what had happened with Shawn, but physically I was fine. I shrugged off the strange symptoms of the previous day.

Two days later, it happened again, this time at work. As I sat in Gary's office talking to him about a printing job, I felt my right foot go numb. *It's happening again,* I thought. I began to try to explain to Gary what was going on.

"Remember the other day when I called you?" I asked him.

He didn't answer. His eyes were focused on my arm; my hand had turned pitch black. "Something's wrong," he said in alarm.

"I think I'll go to the hospital now," I said.

Gary wanted to call an ambulance, but I wouldn't hear of it. He offered to drive me and I protested. I told him I would be ok and I could take care of myself. I walked out of his office, got in my car, and drove myself to the emergency room.

At the ER, the medical staff took one look at me and said, "Hook her up. She's having a stroke." They kept me there for four days. Gary was the first one there and I asked him to find me a phone so I could call my mom. The kids came and stayed as long as the nurse would let them. Gary refused to leave and when I woke up several times through the night, he was still there. He stayed by my side the entire night. The next morning he went and picked up Katy and Nancy and brought them to see me. Mom came with them and they stayed for several hours. He brought the girls in every day I was in the hospital and Mom also came in. He would take them home and come back to sit by my side until the nurses finally told him to go home and get some sleep. The fourth day, I insisted they let me leave. They wanted me to stay in the hospital longer, but I refused. I explained that I had no insurance and no money. The doctors objected. They wanted to perform additional tests. I refused. I packed my bag, signed release papers, and left.

Weeks went by and I had more of these episodes. It was starting to take its toll on me and I was panicked, thinking that I would lose my accounts again if I couldn't pull myself together. Gary was worried sick about me. He had mentioned a few times that he was concerned about me living alone but I shrugged him off, telling him I was ok.

Shawn and Sarah had an apartment nearby and Shawn and I were speaking again. We would be okay in time. He is, in a lot of ways, like me. He never gives up! He has a huge heart and tries to understand things even when they hurt. I love him for that. He and Sarah were also growing as a family and they started going to a counselor who specialized in relationships. Sarah's father was also a very strong influence in Shawn's growth. He was a very wise man and wasn't afraid to share his own failures with Shawn.

Wendy was starting to have trouble with her own marriage. She had come to me and told me a little each visit until she built up a trust with me. The day came when she was finally sharing with me.

Throughout all of this, my health was declining rapidly. I was having mini strokes every week and I also started having seizures. Then the second hospital trip came and another three days and more tests. I was losing this battle and didn't have the strength to keep going. Test after test and still no answers. The doctors were baffled because they couldn't find anything that would be causing the mini strokes. When they released me Gary picked me up and on the ride home he again asked if I wanted to stay with him for a while. I told him that it might be a good idea if I stayed just until I was better. I was scared and I felt like I was leaving this world. I wasn't ready because I had so much left to do. I didn't want to be alone.

"What do I do with my house?" I asked him.

"Give it back," he said. "Tell the guy who owns it you're moving out. Let's get your stuff. Let's move you in."

It took Gary a week to rearrange his home and move my stuff over. At the end of that week, my daughters and I moved into his place. Just like that, a year and a half after my divorce, Gary and I were living together.

It was a little house, but the girls each had their own room. Gary had moved his belongings out of two of the rooms and redone them for Katy and Nancy. Nancy was fine with the move. Katy was not. There was an ongoing battle between them. Nancy liked Gary and felt safe with him. Katy, however, would tell her, "You can't like him."

Over the next six months my health continued to go downhill. I was struggling to keep my accounts alive and trying to maintain my life in a new and strange arrangement. Surprisingly, the kids were handling my living arrangements quite well. Joe wasn't. Whenever the girls visited their dad, they heard more confusing talk. "He's not your Dad," Joe would tell eight-year old Nancy. "You can't like him. He's not your father." She would come home crying.

"Dad says I'm not supposed to love Gary. What do I do?"

I reassured her as best I could.

I spent the next year living with Gary. In so many ways, life was good. My love for Gary continued to grow. Dealing with my children was challenging, but we were managing. Now Shawn and Wendy were both very much in my life.

Time slowly was healing our relationship. Of course there were other issues that came between us, but nothing like the awful experience we had gone through. It was a reminder to Shawn and me every time we argued; we were slowly learning to respect each other and our feelings.

Shawn and Sarah's counseling continued. Sarah was at her wit's end with their relationship—frustrated, hurt and angry, and so was Shawn. They have had a long road together and are still friends. I like that! Both of them are learning so much. My son is a wonderful parent; he is patient, understanding and openly loving with his daughter and so is Sarah. Everyday we learn to trust each other more.

Wendy was contemplating a divorce and confided in me. She told me she signed herself up for the training in Idaho and I couldn't wait for her to go. It meant a chance for us to be closer than she ever allowed. It also meant that there was a chance for happiness, something that Wendy had never really had.

My job was going great. Even with my struggle with health problems I had landed a very large account. I had been working on this account for seven long years. Gary was already in it and kept mentioning the work I did to his buyer. Then it happened, she called me. It was more income than I dreamed I would ever accomplish. I was traveling back and forth to Chicago and loving every minute of it. Gary and I worked side by side on this account; it had been a seven- year process and I loved working with him. He traveled with me when he could. We were a good team and we worked together well. He was there just in case my health let me down, and I was there, in case he had to be in the office.

I continued to have mini-strokes though and my health was deteriorating. Every morning, exhaustion ragged me. During the day I barely had any strength. It took every ounce of determination I had to get up each morning and go to work. I couldn't afford to lose another account, especially not now. I worked too hard and too long to have it fall apart. Gary was always there to pick up the slack for me.

I was experiencing one or two strokes a week. I saw many doctors, but none knew how to diagnose me. They checked my heart and valves. They took EKGs and did MRIs and CAT scans. They checked my head for damage, but found none. In the end, they diagnosed this as a blood disease and simply tried different medications, hoping one would work. My primary care physician finally told me, "This is something you'll need to monitor and manage."

So that's what I did. I worked to keep my stress levels under control. Whenever I got overloaded, I could feel it coming on, and I would let Gary know. He'd help me to calm down.

My remedy became lying down and sleeping through the episode along with the blood thinner. Whenever I did that, I would wake up somewhat refreshed, and the symptoms would be diffused enough that I could keep going. I've learned how to manage my mystery disease over time.

I was maintaining my accounts and life was getting better all the time. I held onto my dreams. Just the way I promised my mom that I would. She called me often and was there every time she knew I needed her. We went for coffee whenever she was in town and caught up on life together. I was nervous when I had to tell her about the fight between Shawn and me. I was still very ashamed that I handled this so badly. She encouraged me to stand strong with him. She also told me that if there were ever such a thing as a perfect mother, kids would never learn a damn thing.

Mom always had a way of making things so much lighter. She laughed after a few minutes and asked me why I didn't knock him out so he couldn't fight back. Still laughing, she stood up and tried to compose herself, telling me that I could sue her for bad parenting. Still giggling she went to bed. The next morning she called Shawn and told him she loved him. That was all she said to him and then she hung up the phone. I didn't get to see her a lot during this last year because Mom had taken a job in her hometown.

With a lot of reluctance she accepted the job there to face some of her own past and try to heal from it. This was very difficult for her not only because it was where she grew up; she took a job at the prison, counseling pedophiles. I was shocked when she told me. She explained that she had to this and why and I understood. Vernal was about 350 miles from where I lived so we would talk for hours on the phone. When I was in the hospital the second time they finally took the phone out of my room because we talked for way to long and the doctor thought I needed my rest. Mom was furious and drove down to Salt Lake City the next day and stayed at my place with the girls again until they released me. Gary wasn't surprised when he showed up to check on the girls again and she was there.

The first time Mom met Gary was when I was in the hospital for the first visit. Gary went to my place to check on the girls and introduced himself to my mom. She told him she had seen him in my room last night when she arrived at the hospital. She looked in and saw I was asleep and so was he, in the chair. She snuck in, kissed me and went to my place to stay with the girls. The first time Mom came to see where I was living and meet Gary formally was her next visit to Salt Lake City. She came and stayed with us for two days and we stayed up all night laughing and talking. She knew by visiting with us that I was happy and she liked him. When she left, she told me how much she loved to watch him smile at me. It reminded her of Dad. The way he would sit back and listen to me talk and smile.

16

CELEBRATION
1999–2000

You deserve the fun, the joy, the freedom, and the pure goodness that flows through the experience of love that indwells you . . . The choice is yours.—David McArthur and Bruce McArthur

$\mathcal{M}$any times I told Gary that I did not want to get married again. After my experiences with my ex-husband, I was marriage-shy. "I love you," I often reassured Gary. "You're my friend. Please don't destroy what we have. Don't ask me to marry you."

I wanted to stay in love. I didn't want marriage to ruin any part of what we had. Our friendship was just too special.

Unlike me, Gary still believed in marriage. Both of us had gone through painful divorces, but he hadn't lost hope. He believed that marriage could work and be beautiful, and with all his heart he wanted to marry me.

One night, Gary took me to a cozy Italian restaurant with white tablecloths and red candles, and our table for two was tucked away in a secluded corner. He ordered a bottle of wine, and I thought he was being romantic.

"I've got something I want to tell you," he said. He reached across the table and gently took both my hands. "Debra Sue Bass," he said, using my maiden name, while he pulled a small case out of his pocket, "Will you marry me?"

Gary opened the case to reveal the most beautiful diamond ring I'd ever seen. I started to cry. Even though he had planned this for months, I had no idea it was coming. It was a romantic, old-fashioned marriage proposal, just like I'd dreamed of when I was very young.

I was shocked, elated, and moved. Despite all my previous reservations and objections, I didn't hesitate.

"Oh my God, yes!" I said. Just like that, it flew out of my mouth.

Gary started to cry. He yelled to the restaurant manager, "She said yes!" The manager and waitress hurried over to our table. We stood up and everyone hugged each other through tears of joy.

The ring was stunning and custom-made. Gary told me he had looked through literally hundreds of diamonds before finding the one he felt sparkled like I did. Talk about romantic!

I watched how the light danced across the diamond. "Wow," I teased Gary, "do I do that?" He answered, "You do it to me every morning. At times I think it's just not real. It spooks me sometimes!"

I had to pinch myself. After enduring so many years of emotional pain, I was finally having a wonderful life. *Was this really happening? Would it last?*

I was a little shy about setting a date when Gary and I talked about the details of our wedding. Gary's enthusiasm won me over, and I realized, why not? Why shouldn't I have that Cinderella wedding I'd always dreamed of? I told Gary that's what I wanted. He smiled. "OK, when?" he asked. I thought about my kids. I thought about Gary's kids. They all needed time to adjust to this. "Well," I replied, "not for at least a year and a half." I saw the look of disappointment on his face.

"Wow, a year and a half . . . " he began. It was March of 2000. He was hoping we'd get married by the end of the year.

"I need to make this okay," I said. "I need this to be okay with my kids." I also needed it to be okay with Gary's kids. Although none of his kids lived at home, and hadn't in a while, he needed to tell them about our plans. They were not happy about me moving in and I knew how they would feel about marriage. Gary didn't want to wait a year and a half, but he knew that it was all very sudden for me. He understood that I needed time to get used to the idea. He also knew my kids would need to adjust to the idea.

My children weren't happy about our engagement, but I knew that in time they'd accept it. In time, they'd see how much Gary and I loved each other. *So what if my children weren't jumping for joy?* At least all of them were in my life again. I was approaching this one step at a time. Mom, on the other hand, was very happy for me; she just wanted to know that I was sure. I told her I hadn't ever been this sure about anything before. She laughed and then told me we had to be nuts—all those kids! Then she told me if anyone could make this work, it was the two of us.

It's all going to work out, I realized. My life was going to be fine. My dreams were becoming reality. I kept what my Mother told me about my dreams very close to my heart because her advice gave me strength.

During the period when I was sick, I spent a lot of time resting in bed. In those quiet moments, I had special visitors: my father and my grandmother, and a host of other spirits who loved me very much. They always showed up quietly and calmly. They were absolutely radiant. On one visit from my grandmother she told me not to worry because it wasn't my time unless I chose it to be. She told me to talk with God and ask to stay for a while. Then she said I was going to write a book about our life. I chuckled at this and she "Yes, my dear, you are." She told me it would help my children and that people I had never met would grow from it. I loved their visits. Even when the room was dark, they would light it up with their luminous essence. I was never alone, which was tremendously comforting. Throughout this time, I also had wonderful conversations with my Dad. He showed me the other side on a few occasions, so I would know what it was like.

153

Often Gary was with me during these visits, and I'd share my spiritual experiences with him as they unfolded. Even though he couldn't see them, not even their glow, he never questioned their presence. He accepted them completely. At times he could feel their presence, especially Dad.

One morning, I was getting ready for work when Dad appeared. He said, very matter-of-factly, "A year and a half? What's wrong with the first of October?"

I replied that I loved October, with its changing leaves and the way the air felt. Dad said, "I know. How about the first?"

I told him, "Okay, in a year and a half."

"No, girl," he insisted. "How about this first of October?" I sat there for a moment, pondering the date. Finally, I agreed. "And you'll be there, won't you, Dad?"

"I wouldn't miss it for the world."

I walked into work that morning and looked into Gary's eyes. "October first," I told him.

"Okay," he replied. "Of what year?"

"This year."

"How can you be so sure?" he asked.

I smiled. "Daddy told me."

It was June when I announced the date to Gary and the next several months I spent carefully planning my wedding. I had my girls help with my plans because I wanted them to be part of all of it. They picked out their dresses and helped me pick out flowers. My four girls and Gary's three girls were in our line and Hokulealani, my granddaughter was the flower girl.

Evan was my matron of honor. Evan's youngest son was our ring bearer. When I told her that Gary had proposed she laughed out loud and said, "I love you, you are doing it. You are making your dreams happen!"

The weeks went by quickly and it was time. I rented two limos—one for Mom and Aunt Betty and the other one for Evan, her boys and my girls. It was a perfect October day. The trees were gorgeous with their changing leaves. Butterflies flitted about. With a high of seventy-six degrees, the temperature was just right. In all my years on Earth, I'd never seen a more beautiful day. It felt like heaven.

I had rented rooms at a lovely bed and breakfast up in the mountains in Midway, Utah, for everyone who was coming to our wedding. Everybody we loved and cared about was there: all of our friends. Gary's family alone was eighty-five people. My family was another fifty, and all of our children. I had even flown in my Aunt Betty to keep my mother company. Their relationship needed to be repaired, and I couldn't think of a better time for healing to take place between Mom and her big sister.

Betty and Lois

This was the first time they'd been together in years. Mom cried when she saw her sister. Over the weekend, the two had a blast together. They shared a huge, beautiful room with two queen beds and a Jacuzzi tub. I pampered them, treating them to a limo ride up the mountain, new outfits and a spa date before the wedding. They both had such fun, and they renewed their relationship.

I smile when I remember how Mom and Aunt Betty flirted with the limousine driver and asked him if he was free for the rest of his life. On the day of my wedding, Mom and Aunt Betty were like schoolgirls, getting their hair and makeup done. Mom wore the beautiful dress I had bought her for the occasion. Mom cried like a little girl when I told her I was getting married; she was so happy for me.

Katy, Nancy, Evan and her boys and I rode up in the other limo.

The girls were still adjusting to the idea of me getting married, but deep down inside they loved Gary and me and they wanted us

Betty, Lois, and Debbie

to be happy. During the limo ride they were giddy with excitement. As we drove up the mountain, Katy had a blast hanging out the window! All the kids were having fun. The family dinner the night before the wedding was beautiful. It is a moment in my heart that will last forever.

I had drawn sketches of my dream dress and found a dressmaker to create it. With its white iridescent sparkles and full skirt, my wedding dress was dazzling.

The next morning I can honestly say I was scared to death. Finally, as the ceremony was starting, I took a deep breath and relaxed into the moment. The wedding was something out of a fairytale, and there was my best friend waiting for me at the end of the aisle with tears in his eyes. I felt my knees giving out, and I felt the strong support from my Shawn walking me down the aisle.

Lois and Debbie

He whispered to me softly, "You're okay, Mom, just keep walking. I have you."

Joy swept me away on this luxuriant fall day and clear October sky. Everyone that I loved was there with me.

My handsome son Shawn held my arm with his strong reassuring grip. I was honored to have him by my side. I stared ahead at my knight, up front, smiling at me. Shawn brought me forward, euphoria lifted me closer, and Gary's eyes carried me the rest of the way to his arms.

We wrote our beautiful ceremony ourselves. Our preacher read a passage from Kahlil Gibran's "The Prophet" that begins like this:

"Your children are not your children.
They are the sons and daughters of Life's longing for itself."

All of our children were mentioned by name. They held hands while the youngest of each family, Gary's daughter Traci and my Nancy, lit the unity candle with trembling hands. That moment symbolized the coming together of two families in one precious flaming light. When the minister announced us as Mr. and Mrs. Gary Williamson I looked out and saw my mother crying, but they were happy tears. Aunt Betty was holding her hand. I watched my children and Gary's as we passed by them looking so confused, but they were there. All I could think of was this is just the beginning, I am going to make it but I'm going to make it big! I'm going to show them they can be happy because I am.

My daughter-in-law's Hawaiian heritage also became an important element of my wedding reception. Her father's Hawaiian band played while he sang exquisitely. The first piece was a tune that was special to my granddaughter and me—it was our song. As he sang "Twinkle, Twinkle Little Star" Hawaiian-style, my sweet Hoku-lealani ran up to me.

"Are you gonna dance with me, Grandma?" she asked.

"Of course I am." My granddaughter and I danced the first dance of the evening. By the end of the song, all my daughters–my three girls, my stepdaughters, and my daughter-in-law–had joined

Hokulealani and Debbie

us. Then it was Gary's turn. The first song was *In This Life,* and the second, *Because You Loved Me.* For the next two songs, he and I danced together, lost in bliss in each other's eyes, as husband and wife.

Some days I wake up in the morning and ask myself, *Is this real?* Wow, this is my life. This is my home. I get on my knees and say, "Thank you."

I love those mornings, and I tell myself, "You did it. All your dreams, they're right here." I'm living proof you can do it. All it took was courage, and the risk to love again.

I have a happy family, a happy marriage. I am living the life I had only dreamed of as a child and the life I wanted my mother and father to have.

Perhaps the greatest reason for my gratitude for my new life is that few women, who like me have been raped or abused for the majority of their lives, can find the courage to take the first step. I am proof that it can happen.

I am living my dreams as though I never completely lost sight of my vision. With a lot of help from people I love and those who have loved me, and even strangers along the way, I have finally reached my dreams. I don't know how I did it, but what matters is that I arrived. Sometimes gifts come to us in a form we don't recognize. When we do finally recognize these as gifts a new door opens to a place we have never seen before. A new beginning is there if you have the courage to go through those doors. When you do, you will find forgiveness and a way to be free from all your hurt. Forgiveness not just for your abuser; it is, most of all, for yourself. It is the way to your dreams. It is a way to be new again.

EPILOGUE: MOM

*R*ecently Mom joined Dad on the other side. I am so thankful we reconciled during this lifetime. For whatever reason, I had blamed her for much of what went wrong in my life. The day came when I realized that she wasn't at fault, and that I missed her. Today I have nothing but love and admiration for her in my heart.

Mom was special. She used to describe to me a beautiful place of fairies and flowers, a safe place she retreated to, particularly in her dreams. Together we watched the movie *"Return to Neverland,"* and I asked her if her place was like what we saw on the big screen.

"Yes, that's where I go," she replied. "You know the fairies, don't you?"

I couldn't resist the chance to tease her a little for all the times she'd warned me not to tell others about my angels. "Yeah, Mom, but don't tell anybody. They'll think you're wacko." She giggled.

Mom was definitely psychic and spiritual. She had the ability to sense what others couldn't. Time and again throughout my life, I'd be at home, in a world of pain for one reason or another and the phone would ring. Invariably, Mom knew her daughter was hurting.

When I left Joe, she knew, even though I hadn't told her. "I knew the minute you walked out that door," she explained. "I could feel it."

She had a remarkable way of feeling what I was feeling, and she never gave up trying to help me. Mom told me, "You have this gift

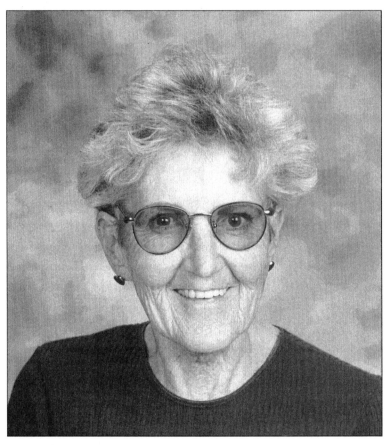

Lois

that you try to deny. Because you don't know what to do with it, it's making you sick. You're absorbing everybody's pain. You've been that way since you were a little girl."

Throughout the course of my life, she had tried to teach me how to let go, how to release all that pain, but I didn't get it. I held it inside me for so many years that it began to consume me. Mom said, "I want you to promise me you will find somebody who can teach you how to release it before it kills you."

I found someone, a very spiritual woman who showed me exactly what I was doing. Step by step, she walked me through how to release and unwind all the pain in my life. Thanks to the techniques she taught me, I was able to get a handle on my sickness and accept my gift of empathy.

Mom never gave up on me. She waited patiently until I was ready to let her back into my life. She was right there by my side anytime I needed her. And she was willing to teach me about the subtle, spiritual side, once I was willing to listen.

Many times Dad had told me that Mom was special. I didn't see it back then. My anger blinded me to her gifts. But I'm glad it took less than a lifetime to reconcile and be friends with her. Dad was right; she is special.

Gifts get passed down from generation to generation, and Mom saw that Wendy had special abilities. When my daughter was a year and a half, Mom tried to warn me. She wanted to protect her granddaughter from cruel people, just as she had tried to protect me when she told me not to talk to others about my angels.

"Wendy has special friends," she said.

"I know, Mom."

"You need to tell her to keep it to herself."

"Mom, don't do that to her," I protested. "We've been down this route before. It's okay. Please let her be with her special people."

"They're angels, you know," Mom informed me.

"I know, Mom."

That was my mother's turning point. She stopped trying to hide or block these wonderful gifts we all had. A few years ago, she asked Wendy, "Are your angels still with you?"

Wendy smiled at her grandmother. "They'll always be with me, Grandma," she replied.

Mom cried a little. "I'm glad," she told my daughter. "I'm glad you didn't make them go away."

Christmas was the last time I saw Mom. She drove up to be with us despite her battle with serious illness. I was anxious for her to be here. I asked her about writing our story again as I did for the last year, 'Mom, are you ready?" Her smile revealed a yes.

I explained to her we were getting together in California on the 29th of January with Aunt Betty to go over details.

"I will be there." Mom told me, but she never made it. Mom went home on the 1st of January. Although I never felt or saw her after Mom's passing, my Aunt Betty had a dream about Mom in heaven with Dad. It was the morning of mom's birthday, January 19, when Aunt Betty called me.

In Betty's dream, Dad was building Mom's dream house, the one she never had here on earth. I listened and cried while Betty shared her dream.

Twenty minutes later, my oldest daughter, Wendy, called me to say that Grandpa was building Grandma a house.

"Wendy, how do you know that?

"Grandma came to see me this morning and told me she was okay." When I shared Wendy's phone call with Aunt Betty she was stunned.

I was not surprised as Dad has been in connection with me from the other side ever since he left this world. I am still waiting patiently to feel Mom's gentle presence. Until then, I have my memories and the lessons my Mother left to me, and to the next generation as well.

Shawn has followed in his grandmother's footsteps. He is now working with foster children along with his wife, Sarah. Together they have two beautiful children, Hokulealani and Easy Boy, and now a little boy waiting to arrive.

Shawn's family

Wendy is traveling with her love, Corey, working as a pharmacist assistant and going to school to be a pharmacist. She is finally happy and loving being in love.

Wendy and Corey

Katy has married a boy who she fell head over heals for. Nicholaus is a hero in our family. He has just returned home after sixteen months in Afghanistan. Katy and Nick have three beautiful children, Alexia, Ryan and Zachary, a little soul who just arrived.

Katy's family

Miss Nancy is just starting high school and on her way to something big! We aren't sure yet what it will be, but with Nancy it is sure to be big.

Nancy and Frodo

Their father is well and happy with someone new.

Me . . . I am happy for the first time in my life. I have love!

Debbie and Gary

I have my memories of Dad and our unsaid words together.

I have the memories of Grandma and her tea parties and banana cream pie; the way she would make chicken noodle soup that you would swear made the whole world a better place; how you could always find God in her jars of buttons.

And I have Mom, in my heart for now and always.

Debbie Williamson tours the United States speaking to groups about overcoming the effects of abuse. She and her husband are the parents of 9 children and 11 grandchildren. After generations of abuse, Debbie's courage stopped the cycle before it was allowed to affect the next generation.

Born in Salt Lake City, she grew up in southern California and now lives in Utah with her family and four miniature schnauzers. Family is her number one priority and when not working with university and church groups, she can often be found golfing and sailing with her children and husband, Gary.